VIETNAM:

Crisis
of
Conscience

ROBERT MCAFEE BROWN
ABRAHAM J. HESCHEL
MICHAEL NOVAK

VIETNAM

Crisis of Conscience

ASSOCIATION PRESS
BEHRMAN HOUSE
HERDER AND HERDER
NEW YORK

VIETNAM: *Crisis of Conscience*

First Printing, June, 1967
Second Printing, August, 1967

Association Press
291 Broadway, New York, N.Y. 10007
Behrman House, Inc.
1261 Broadway, New York, N.Y. 10001
Herder and Herder, Inc.
232 Madison Avenue, New York, N.Y. 10016

Publisher's stock numbers: paper, 1649p; cloth, 1656
Library of Congress catalog card number: 67-21994
PRINTED IN THE UNITED STATES OF AMERICA

Contents

INTRODUCTION 7

I. STUMBLING INTO WAR AND STUMBLING OUT (MICHAEL NOVAK) 11
The Three Levels of the Argument 12
The Meaning of the Cold War 14
China and Southeast Asia 20
Vietnam 24
The First Stages 28
Afraid of Four Hundred Men 31
America Takes Over 34
Inheriting A Moral Nightmare 36
Why We Have Done It 41
The Values We Stand For 46

II. THE MORAL OUTRAGE OF VIETNAM (ABRAHAM J. HESCHEL) 48
Military Victory—A Moral Defeat 52
Has Our Conscience Become a Fossil? 56
Is War an Answer to Human Agony? 57
The Crisis of Responsibility 59

III. AN APPEAL TO THE CHURCHES AND SYNAGOGUES (ROBERT MCAFEE BROWN) 62
The Need to Speak 65
The Increasing Anguish 67
Clearing Away the Underbrush—Or, How Not to Think About Vietnam 77
The Search for Alternatives 85
How Can We Make Our Intent Credible to Others? 89
Specific Tasks for Churches and Synagogues 97
Our Ongoing Responsibility 105

APPENDIX 107
Statement of the Synagogue Council of America, January, 1966 109

Statement of the Central Committee of the World Council of Churches, meeting in Geneva, February 8-17, 1966 111
Excerpts from the Encyclical *Christi Matri* of Pope Paul VI, September 15, 1966 113
Statement of the American Roman Catholic Bishops, meeting in Washington, November, 1966 114
Excerpts from "An Appeal to the Churches Concerning Vietnam," issued by the General Assembly of the National Council of Churches, December 9, 1966 118

SELECTED BIBLIOGRAPHY 123

Introduction

The pages that follow grow out of our shared concern that our nation is embroiled in a conflict in Vietnam which we find it impossible to justify, in the light of either the message of the prophets or the gospel of Jesus of Nazareth. We feel that our churches and synagogues have been unwilling to face the moral implications of that conflict. We believe that even those who have supported the United States intervention in Vietnam must come to grips with what the United States is actually doing to that nation. This book is a plea to all Americans—committed, hesitant, uncertain—to confront the terrible realities of the war in Vietnam, before it is too late.

While we address our plea primarily to those within the churches and synagogues, we also address it to all men of goodwill, whatever faith they hold. If they have already confronted the moral issues of Vietnam, we hope this book will reinforce their concern to continue doing so. If they have not faced those issues, we hope that it will help them to do so, and that whether they emerge agreeing with us or not, they will try to articulate their own position in a conscientious public manner. We urge that those who have no involvement in Catholicism, Protestantism, or Judaism join forces with us in practical steps wherever they can, and that in addition they continue to goad the churches and synagogues into responsibility. "You, of all people," they have every right to say, "should be trying to provide leadership on this primary and inescapable moral problem of our time." In any case, we wish to lay particularly upon the conscience of the religious community the fact that it has lagged behind others in the country and the probability that in the weeks ahead fateful decisions are likely to be made by our government for good or for ill.

The occasion of the book was the attendance of each of us at a clergy mobilization in Washington, January 31-February 1, 1967, sponsored by Clergy and Laymen Concerned About Vietnam. After two days of meetings with congressmen and with representatives of the State Department, the White House, and the Defense Department, we found ourselves converging in the feeling that the policymakers frequently wish it were politically feasible to do other than they are doing, but that they have no assurance that the country as a whole would back them if they were, for example, to engage in bold initiatives for a negotiated peace. Our desire, therefore, is to provide a sufficient treatment of the political and moral dimensions of the Vietnam issue that those who agree with us will offer public support for a change in policy, a public support strong enough to make itself felt in Washington. If the churches and synagogues cannot take the lead in creating this new climate of opinion, then we seriously wonder how they can continue to deserve the respect of men of conscience within them or outside them.

If it seems to some readers that a book addressed to the churches and synagogues should be more "religious" in tone and vocabulary, we can only respond that any discussion of how men live and die is a theological, moral, and religious discussion, regardless of phraseology. If it seems to other readers that a book on such a subject can be written only by experts in political science, politics, and history, we can only respond that in a democracy like ours it is still the civic responsibility of every man (once he has studied the issues and listened to the experts) to raise his voice so that his government cannot miss it.

We have for many months, even years, read as widely about the Vietnam war as possible and have submitted the present manuscript to experts. We have tried to do our homework solidly and well. The pressures of time under which we wrote the final draft were, however, cruel. Moreover, even as we wrote, events were happening, during February, 1967, that revealed how many impossible conditions surround our government's pledge of "unconditional negotiations." (See Theodore Draper, "How Not to Negotiate," *The New York Review of Books,* May 4, 1967.) And in March and April our government escalated the war almost weekly, in direct contradiction to earlier pledges. General Westmoreland returned from the field in April to make political speeches which purveyed a simplistic and, according to our researches, false interpretation of the political issues at stake in Vietnam. Our shame and sorrow grew daily, though our words were already being frozen in print.

Our division of labor is clear from the table of contents. Michael Novak introduces the discussion by sketching the historical development of our present involvement in Vietnam and the moral dilemmas that involvement poses for us. Abraham J. Heschel makes a plea to the conscience of the individual to shake off the moral numbness that has surrounded our approach to Vietnam. Robert McAfee Brown suggests ways in which the churches and synagogues can make a more effective corporate witness to bring about changes in our policy, developing many of the points mentioned briefly in the "position paper" presented at the Washington mobilization. The appendix includes a brief sampling of statements by leading Protestant, Catholic, and Jewish bodies, to indicate that part of our task is simply to catch up with our own leadership.

We represent three major religious traditions in the United States—Catholicism, Protestantism, and Judaism. On many issues we are divided, but on the issue of Vietnam we are not. We feel that the moral urgency of Vietnam is so great that we must speak together rather than separately, and we urge all of our fellow Americans to do the same. In one sense, of course, we can speak only for ourselves, since we represent no one "officially." But in a deeper sense, we are sure we speak for many of our fellow Americans who are as pained and sorrowing as we, but have heretofore not found a way to articulate their pain and sorrow. We hope we speak for millions.

ROBERT MCAFEE BROWN
ABRAHAM J. HESCHEL
MICHAEL NOVAK

Note: Clergy and Laymen Concerned About Vietnam, 475 Riverside Drive, New York, New York 10027, is an interfaith group seeking to coordinate national efforts among the Catholic, Protestant, and Jewish communities to bring about a change of policy in Vietnam. Royalties from the sale of this book are being given to it.

I. Stumbling Into War and Stumbling Out

by MICHAEL NOVAK

To apply religious language to political affairs is always dangerous. Religion speaks the language of benediction and condemnation, of ultimate values and ultimate purposes, of the holy and of mystery, of moral right and of moral abomination. The language of politics, however, is the language of power, interest, probabilities, strategies, results. It may be possible for religious people to be realists; it may be possible for men of politics to be holy. But it is not common to find either one of these possibilities realized. It is difficult to be a Christian or a Jew; it is difficult to be a man of politics. To be both at once is not difficulty doubled but difficulty squared.

Nevertheless, American Christians and Jews find themselves today involved in bloodshed, terror, and destruction in the distant nation of Vietnam. Whether they have wished it or not, their government in their name is participating in one of the four or five most destructive wars in all history. The fire power already exercised is enormous—more shells fired in a single engagement in a single night than in whole wars (as General Dayan of Israel recently reported from the scene). Christians and Jews are not anxious to be known as men of blood, but as men of peace. No wonder that this war, seen every evening on their television screens, makes them uneasy. No wonder they see in it a contradiction between their aspirations and their practice. They would like America to be creative; they experience it as destructive.

The war in Vietnam involves millions of persons in crises of conscience. Young men, who would not hesitate were it another Hitler to be opposed, another World War II, wonder whether they can conscientiously fight in *this* war. Those who live near napalm factories wonder whether they can bear to live in such a neighborhood without protesting the inhumanity of that sticky, flaming weapon. Taxpayers, citizens who do not know what to believe in conflicting reports about the war, wives and parents of soldiers, those who work in the military or defense industries, those concerned with the millions of displaced persons in South Vietnam—all wonder what is demanded of *them*, as this war creeps on from day to day.

Moreover, the more the people know about the background and the conduct of this war, the less many of them like it. Those who study events in Southeast Asia in this century, and particularly the history of the United States involvement in the affairs of Vietnam, seem to be those most pained and most shamed by the continuance of the war.

Yet the issues involved in this war are among the most complicated ever faced by citizens of the United States. Few persons—even among the most thoroughly informed—are perfectly clear about what is right or wrong, or about what is to be done. There are many issues on which reasonable men disagree. It is important to isolate as many of those issues as possible. Above all, it is important for as many American religious men as possible to come to see exactly what is being done in their name. It is crucial that basic information become widely known. For political life in the United States is so constituted that each of us is responsible for what our government does. If our government does evil, we are implicated. Exactly in proportion as we are a free and responsible people, we are guilty of what is done in our name. It will not be possible, later on, for people of intelligence to plead ignorance. We will not be able to say "But we didn't realize!" The information is available, though effort must be expended to acquire it. That effort may be the means of our salvation.

The Three Levels of the Argument

In general, there is not much dialogue between liberals and conservatives in American politics. In general, their arguments shoot right by each other, without ever touching. The same is true of the hawks and the doves in the present war. Everyone wants peace, but some want it through the application of greater violence and some want it through the diminution of violence. Neither side listens clearly to what the other side is saying; the arguments seldom join. Perhaps 10 per cent of the American people desire the United States simply to withdraw from South Vietnam; perhaps another 10 per cent desire the United States to destroy North Vietnam and even to carry the war to China if necessary, in order to destroy "the Communists" while they are still weak. But what about the other 80 per cent, torn this way and that by argument, hesitation, and doubt? Here is where the power in America lies. Here is where there is much goodness and decency, but also much shirking of responsibility. Here is where there is an information gap. It is to that 80 per cent that the following discussion is addressed.

There are at least three levels of discussion in the argument about the war in Vietnam. The first concerns the meaning of the cold war in general; the second concerns the role of China in Southeast Asia; the third concerns the meaning of the civil war in Vietnam. On each of these levels men disagree. It is not surprising, then, that arguments about the role of the United States in South Vietnam are often inconclusive. Often the basic source of disagreement is on the first of these levels, at other times on the second, and sometimes on the third. Moreover, those who argue about these important matters often fail to make clear what their presuppositions are at each of these prior levels. No wonder that reasonable men fail to understand each other in such a wilderness of disputed facts and interpretations.

It will be impossible for me, in a short essay, to do justice to every point on every side of the discussion at each level of the argument. What I propose to do instead is to mark out the various levels clearly, to bring into relief the many ambiguities and sources of disagreement, and to state as cogently as possible my own views at each stage. It will not be possible for me to state fully the arguments of those who disagree with me; but I hope to be fair to those who disagree, and to make it easy for them to point out exactly where the differences between us lie. My aim, in short, is not to exhort or to plead, far less to condemn. My aim is to mark out the terrain clearly, and to advance step by step through it as

I do so. Since I have gradually come to a position of my own, I cannot be neutral; but I can hope to be both clear and fair. My aim, then, is not so much to persuade as to clarify.

The Meaning of the Cold War

The first level of discussion concerns the general meaning of the cold war. For those with a very simple theology, this meaning is limpid. It is good guys versus bad guys, the godly versus the ungodly, the forces of light against the forces of barbarism. For such persons, the battle we face in our century is a battle for civilization itself, and the antagonists are the "slave nations" and the nations of the "free world." For them, "Communists" war against "anti-Communists," barbarians threaten civilized peoples, law and order, and the American way of life. Such persons think of the world in blocs. Their view of history is apocalyptic, just because the issue is so clear: there is a titanic struggle between two huge, powerful forces. For such persons, the cold war will last until one side or the other is defeated. Compromise and peaceful coexistence merely postpone the day of reckoning and confuse the fundamental issue.

It is possible that one reason why some Americans are prone to accepting this simple view of world affairs is reflected in the American passion for television and cinematic "westerns." In cowboy stories, one side is always clearly distinguished from the other side—sometimes even by the color of their hats. One side fights for law and order, the other side is lawless. If the plot includes Indians, racial overtones are usually present; then the conflict is between savages (nonwhites) and civilized, peace-loving pioneers (whites, who represent the forces of progress). The showdown almost always comes through violence. Those win who have the more sophisticated weapons or the faster draw. Moreover, even when the bad guys outnumber the good guys, the good guys calmly rely upon greater fire power or technical skill. The good guys always win. It is disgraceful to compromise. When, temporarily, the bad guys wipe out a group of good guys, it is a cruel and heartless massacre; when the good guys kill huge numbers of bad guys, it is a victory for justice and civilization.

The myth of the good cowboy or the pure and hardy pioneer is only reinforced by the simplistic employment of biblical categories of light and darkness, virtue and vice, the redeemed and the unredeemed. God favors the pure of heart, who are also, in the main, the white of skin. The blood of one white man is, somehow, more sacred than the blood of many savages. It is important, in the myth, to keep a kind of "body count." When too many whites die, anxiety rises and the balance must be redressed by punishment so severe that the nonwhites are reduced until they are no longer a numerical threat.

Perhaps it is a mistake, so early in this discussion, to bring this racial factor out into the open. Most Americans do not seem to be aware of it. When it is stated starkly, we are inclined to disown it. But if we reflect upon the unspoken meaning of a thousand images that have bombarded us since our youth—in stories, books, political harangues, movies, magazines, and even dreams—perhaps many of us will admit, sadly, that the myth is powerful among us. The history of the treatment afforded by white Americans to the Indians, Negroes, Mexicans, Chinese, and even Latin peoples, does not allow us to deny it speedily.

In any case, even apart from its racial overtones, the cold war is envisaged by some Americans in stark and shocking simplicity. Some Americans seem to *need* a single, easily identified enemy. In our day, "communism" supplies that need. (How delighted some people appear when denouncing the foe, how exultant and released!)

But the issue of the cold war is complicated for many other Americans precisely because Communists *do* speak of an international movement, refer to one another as "comrade," write enthusiastically of secrecy and conspiracy, and envisage—they, too—the world in blocs as a confrontation between darkness and light. In brief, there are those on both sides of the cold war who delight in the apocalyptic style, and who thrive on the division of all human beings into two rival camps. Moreover, as long as Moscow remained the undisputed head of the world Communist movement, and as long as it suited the postwar situation for "satellite nations" to be subservient to Moscow, Communist nations did tend to act as one single "orbit."

On January 30, 1967, former Ambassador George F. Kennan testified before the Senate Foreign Relations Committee:

> To attribute today to the various parties, regimes and factions that make up the world Communist movement any sort of a unified political personality—to speak of them as though they represented a single disciplined force, operating under the conspiratorial control of a single political will, as I sometimes still hear people speak of them in this country . . . is to fly in the face of an overwhelming body of evidence, to move intellectually in the realm of patent absurdity, to deny by implication the relevance of external evidence to the considerations and decisions of foreign affairs. The unity of the Communist bloc is a matter of the past; and it will not be restored. This Humpty Dumpty will not and cannot be reassembled.
>
> Now this, of course, does not mean that there is no problem. These regimes and factions remain Communist, or nominally Communist, even if they are not united. . . . But here there are certain circumstances that we must be careful to bear in mind.
>
> First of all, what Communism means today embraces a very wide spectrum of outlooks and behavior. Some of these Communist elements, like the Chinese Communist regime, present from our standpoint as ugly and menacing a phenomenon as did Lenin's Russia at the height of its world-revolutionary enthusiasm.
>
> Others, as in the case of the Yugoslav regime or the Italian Communist party, are operating on the basis of concepts which present no greater problems from our standpoint than those that govern the behavior of many regimes or parties that do not call themselves Communist at all. It is simply impossible to generalize, today, about Communism as a problem in the spectrum of American foreign policy.
>
> But in addition to that, even within the framework of the individual Communist parties or regimes, the nature of Communism is not a static thing. It has already undergone great changes in many instances, and is still in a process of change everywhere.[1]

[1] *New York Times,* January 31, 1967.

How, then, shall we think of the cold war? It is realistic to recall that 90 per cent of the world's people do not eat as well as Americans, or live in homes like ours, or drive our automobiles. Yet these peoples, through cinema and television and radio, have caught a glimpse of what is possible for them. The shackles of thousands of years of poverty have been broken. Ignorance can be ended. Frightful dictatorships, tyrannies, caste systems, and the lordly ways of the rich can at last be overcome. The whole human race is astir with hope and rising expectations. It is this factor, more than any other, that brings about the instability which we have called "the cold war." The enemy is hunger, disease, ignorance and poverty. Social, political, and economic revolutions have been—and are—desperately needed in almost all quarters of the world.

Communism and modified capitalism are two rival strategies for dealing with this revolutionary age. Both the United States and Russia promise to help the poor and the needy efficiently and swiftly. Each has been willing to fight the other in the race to help the other nations of the world. Both seek to extend their own power and to protect their own security, at the expense of smaller nations, yet while aiding those smaller nations. But in the clash of these two powers, one should not lose sight of the mutual enemy of both of them: poverty, lack of industry, corrupt feudal governments, hunger. The first issue in the cold war is human welfare. The clash between communism and modified capitalism is a secondary issue, set in the context of the first.

Moreover, to speak of the great power of the United States and of Russia is misleading. There is a tendency for people to think of the world in only two blocs—Russia's friends and ours. Such a tendency is not supple enough to cope with the reality of world affairs, for in reality independent nations and the spirit of nationalism are increasingly active. It is not accurate to lump all the "free nations" together; they include many different kinds of governments, economies, and self-interests. It is just as inaccurate to lump all the "Communist" nations together. The adjective has become more important than the noun: Chinese Communists differ strenuously with Russian Communists; the North Vietnamese Communists cherish ancient animosities against the

Chinese; Albanian Communists differ sharply from their neighbors, the Yugoslavs.

It should not surprise us, then, that our response to each new problem with a Communist nation may need to be different from the last. Each situation may well be different. It would be a great error to think that we can "learn from history" simply by doing now what we should have done five years ago. What we need most to learn from history is the need for flexibility and accurate, timely analysis. Worse than making one mistake is to correct it just when the time for the correction has passed. We must meet each new situation on its own terms, keeping the past in mind but not being predetermined by it. Rigidity of mind is not an asset during a revolutionary period. Calmness and the clear perception of differences are, by contrast, extraordinarily helpful.

Again, it is helpful to rid our minds of conspiratorial thinking. Each nation has its own interests; collisions are inevitable. Revolutions and wars have occurred almost monthly since 1945; the amazing fact is that so few of them have proved serious or widened into greater conflagrations. There are plenty of reasons for wars and revolutions in an age such as ours, when peoples on all continents have suddenly been awakened to what human life could be like. There is no need to think that every disturbance is caused by Communist agents—or agents of the CIA. In the words of former Ambassador Kennan:

> It must never be forgotten that in the pattern of our relationship with any great nation there are always elements of conflict in outlook as in interest. An uncomplicated relationship between great nations does not exist, has never existed, and will never exist.
>
> In the tensions that have agitated the relations between our country and the Soviet Union over the half century of the latter's existence, there have always been, for this reason, two components: one that arose from the peculiar ideological outlooks and commitments of the Soviet leaders—from their quality, in other words, as Communist; the other one composed of the abundant frictions, suspicions, anxieties and conflicts of interest that normally

> bedevil the relations between great states and do not constitute in themselves a proper source for discouragement or despair with relation to the prospects for world peace.
>
> I think it may safely be said that, in the pattern of our differences with the Soviet leadership over the course of the past fourteen years, that component which reflects the nature of the Communist ideological commitments has tended generally to decline; and the relative importance of the other component, the normal one, has tended, accordingly, to rise. . . . It may be helpful to think about Russia as simply another great world power with its own interests and concerns, often necessarily in conflict with our own but not tragically so—a power different in many respects, but perhaps no longer in essential ones from what Russia would have been had there been no Communist revolution in that country fifty years ago.[2]

Finally, it is important to remember that communism is, in part, what we make it. Our policies and deeds affect those of other countries. There are conflicts within every nation in which communism has taken root. By our initiatives, we strengthen one party in this conflict and embarrass the other. It would be useful if we could learn to help the more pragmatic and less ideological leaders, the more peaceful and less belligerent leaders, by the flexibility and clarity of our own actions. Thus Kennan said:

> Not only does international Communism present itself to us today in many diverse aspects, and not only is it a phenomenon constantly in process of change; it is also something that reacts sensitively in many respects to what we do and say, and must therefore be regarded as partially subject to our influence.
>
> Almost everywhere in the Communist world there are forces more inclined to appreciate the values of a peaceful world and to contribute, where they can, to development in that direction, and there are forces less inclined to move along this line. We have it in our power, by the manner in which we frame our policies, to encourage or

[2] *Ibid.*

to discourage either of these conflicting forces. International Communism is thus not just entirely what we find it to be. It is in part what we make of it.[3]

We would be foolish to fail to notice the encouraging signs in the evolution of communism during the last twenty years. We are no longer dealing with "the naive world-revolutionary force of Lenin's day or with the grim monolith of Soviet power that confronted us in the days of Stalin."[4] The tragedy is that so many Americans prefer to believe that communism has not changed since Lenin and Stalin; they seem to take pleasure in making their boogeyman as vicious as possible. They do not like flexibility or complexity; they prefer their issues black-and-white. If they want a showdown badly enough, the danger is, they may get it. A great deal depends, then, on the emergence of enough Americans willing to make distinctions, and to meet each new situation on its own terms, as realistically and perceptively as possible.

To sum up: the main issue of the cold war is rapid social, political, and economic development among the vast majority of the world's people. The main enemies are hunger, poverty, ignorance, disease. Communism and modified capitalism are two rival strategies for coping with these necessary and inevitable revolutions of our age. But neither communism nor modified capitalism are monoliths; both are capable of indefinite evolution and development, according to the individual genius of each nation. The more diversity and open development our government can promote by its flexible conduct in world affairs, the more it will assist in the evolution of communism in a direction compatible with the interests and hopes and safety of our own people and all others. Now is not the time for rigidity; it is time for wisdom.

China and Southeast Asia

It is never a mistake in analyzing political affairs to look first at the factors of power. When one looks at Southeast Asia, the overwhelming fact is the power of China. No other nation in the area rivals her in military power, inner dynam-

[3] *Ibid.*
[4] *Ibid.*

ism, or political unrest. For the next ten years, it appears, China is the great power among other world powers on whom those who cherish freedom and peace must fix their gaze.

But it is important to be realistic in assessing the power of China. Because little is known of her, because she has been isolated from the rest of the world, the tendency to endow her with fantasy and myth is unusually strong. The achievement of Mao Tse-tung in carrying through his revolution and in organizing such immense numbers of people only contributes to this tendency. Moreover, the military power exhibited by the Chinese in Korea surprised and shocked the United States. News that China is on the threshold of possessing operational nuclear missiles heightens the specter of the country's power.

Furthermore, the Chinese political style is quite unlike the style familiar to us. Hordes of chanting youths, mass revolutionary fervor, enforced collectivization, secrecy, and recent political feuding—all these things make China appear to us like "an enigma wrapped in mystery."

Consequently, the first rule of sensible dealing with China would seem to be this: Remind yourself that all the ingredients of fantasy and bad melodrama are here present in abundance. Almost everything conspires to make us think of the Chinese as less than human, or perhaps as more than human. Since we know so little about what they are like, and since what we do know seems to show them as very unlike us, we find ourselves groping in a kind of darkness. We seem to be dealing with vague images and abstractions, instead of with human beings whom we can recognize, with whom we can sympathize, whose aspirations and actions we can readily understand.

But some things about China do seem clear. Her population is the largest in Asia, and is increasing at an extraordinarily rapid pace. This fact alone marks her as a power that must be reckoned with. Besides, her revolution came much later than the Russian revolution, and the much-revered leaders of that revolution are still in power. Thirdly, her leaders—and especially Mao—seem intent upon *not* following the path of Russia. In Mao's eyes, the Russians have become too much like the rest of the world. Moreover, the younger generation of Chinese lacks a bitter revolutionary experience; they have inherited the revolution too easily. For such reasons, Mao seems intent upon exercising "the Red Guard," turning them loose upon his opponents in the country who are already, like the Russians before them, abandoning the ideological ways of communism in favor of pragmatism, prosperity, and peace.

With each year that passes, internal strife in China seems to reach a higher pitch. For the situation of China has changed in the last twenty years, but key ideas of Mao, it appears, have not. The opposition to him, according to press reports in early 1967, is formidable beyond the earlier expectations of anyone outside China.

Yet it has been argued for some time that internal tensions within China would require her leaders to find diversion and to stimulate patriotism by foreign adventures. But here the Chinese have been restrained and judicious. They have preferred to talk loudly and to do little. They have blustered about "wars of liberation," but they have been very careful not to become implicated themselves. They have not seriously molested Macao or Hong Kong—much closer to them than the Dominican Republic or Cuba to the United States. (Macao and Hong Kong are important to them for foreign exchange.) They were restrained in their attempt to clarify a disputed boundary with India. They ventured a large-scale military involvement only in Korea and used military means in Tibet to reacquire territory Chinese have long believed theirs.

In Vietnam, however, the Chinese at first seemed to score a political advantage, without the commitment of a single unit of their own troops. They have watched the destruction of the Vietnamese nation, an ancient and traditional enemy on their southern flank. They have watched the huge involvement and increasing frustration of the United States, the world power they fear most. They have inhibited the flow of Russian aid to North Vietnam, and have given relatively little aid themselves. But, increasingly, the vital interests of China herself have come to be seriously endangered. The threat of huge U.S. bases so close to her own territory enkindles the patriotic ardor of her own people.

Moreover, in regard to the United States presence in Vietnam, the Chinese leaders have been rational and clear in their statement of their own aims. They have said they will not become involved unless the United States invades North

Vietnam, or trespasses upon Chinese soil. It may even be fair to say that Chinese intentions are clearer than American intentions, for the United States government has as yet set no uppermost limits on possible military escalation. Of course, it is often politically wise not to announce limits to one's intentions in advance. The danger, however, is the risk of miscalculation.

This danger in regard to China is heightened by a basic ambiguity in United States policy. Richard N. Goodwin, former special assistant to Presidents Kennedy and Johnson, has testified that the United States has not had a clear policy regarding China.[5] Bernard Fall added: "But the truth is that nobody has really made up his mind in Washington as to whether it is a straight *Chinese* expansionist threat that has to be contained or whether it is militant *Communism* that has to be contained. This perhaps explains why the Vietnam problem is such a muddle."[6] Is the United States really afraid of *China* and Chinese *nationalism?* In that case, Vietnam may not be the place to be bogged down. Or is the United States really afraid of the spread of "*communism*"*?* In that case, the United States would be involved in Vietnam even if the Chinese have nothing to do with it.

But even apart from Vietnam, the United States does not seem to have a clear policy in regard to China. It is one thing to fear Chinese nationalism, fed by an exploding population in the first phases of industrialization. (The Chinese have never controlled all of Asia—not even all of Indochina. Bernard Fall has written of the national museum in North Vietnam, where young children in red scarves are proudly shown how their nation has for two thousand years resisted the Chinese.) It is another thing to fear the mystique of Communist ideology. Too much fear on our part of a rising tide of communism would represent the greatest victory that Communist propaganda has ever scored. For mere boasts do not make a genuine threat; they merely frighten the unrealistic.

On the other hand, the Chinese have every reason to resent and to fear the presence of huge new American bases so near their borders. White men from the West have come as imperialists to Asia for many generations now. The Chi-

---

[5] *Commentary,* May, 1966.

[6] *Ibid.*

nese have little reason to believe that the United States is more benevolent than other white men have been. Moreover, since the Chinese have staked their destiny upon Maoist principles, it is unlikely that they have confidence in the aims of a nation like ours. Many besides the Chinese think the United States will do all it can to halt native revolutions of any kind, in the attempt to maintain a stable world order. The present world order is very profitable for capitalists in the United States, who are sitting on top of the heap. The foreign aid given by the United States to underdeveloped nations is regarded as a new kind of imperialism: not military but dollar imperialism. Dollar imperialism is not as obvious as colonial imperialism; it does not attempt to set up a colonial political office. Instead, it (at least in effect) buys out willing native politicians and interferes in the country through economic rather than political methods. It is just as effective as colonial imperialism, though harder to unmask. (Americans don't think of themselves as imperialists; or, if so, only as humanitarian imperialists.) China has no Monroe Doctrine for keeping alien nations out of Asia, although she might like to have such a doctrine.

Finally, the apparent bitterness of the Chinese against the Russians no longer, as of April, 1967, works in favor of a settlement in Vietnam. The Chinese are again allowing the shipment of Russian arms to North Vietnam by way of China. China sits upon the borders of North Vietnam as Russia does not. The Chinese influence upon the North Vietnamese has an authority that cannot be overlooked. Yet P. J. Honey reports[7] that, since 1957, the North Vietnamese have doctrinally parted ways with China and, since 1960, have sided increasingly with Russia, the main source of their material aid. Our deeds in Vietnam now force China and Russia together.

Vietnam

The recent history of the nation of Vietnam is sad and bitter. The United States, after supplying Ho Chi Minh and his capable guerrillas and working closely with them since

[7] In *Communism in North Vietnam* (Cambridge: M.I.T. Press, 1963).

late in the Second World War, allowed French colonialism in Vietnam to be renewed. Senator George McGovern noted[8] that it is difficult to see why the United States supported French colonialism, while urging the British to leave Malaysia and India and the Dutch to leave Indonesia, and withdrawing U.S. rule from the Philippines. Worse, as Arthur M. Schlesinger, Jr., reports,[9] the United States began to pay the costs of the French war against our former Vietnamese allies. By 1954, the United States was paying for 80 per cent of the French war effort against the Vietnamese. Ho Chi Minh had always admired the American Revolution of 1776; George Washington was one of his political heroes and the words of our Declaration of Independence appeared in the Declaration of Independence of Vietnam. American conduct must now seem inscrutable and devious to him. At the battle of Dienbienphu, President Eisenhower contemplated sending bombers to the defense of the surrounded French, in order to break the Vietnamese seige; Senator Lyndon Johnson firmly refused to endorse military intervention.

In 1954, the Vietnamese learned that those who fight in a just cause can win a war of attrition, even if it lasts ten years. The French were not decisively defeated in the fight. But the French people could no longer support a colonial war. Because of divided opinion at home, the French army had to be withdrawn.

But the Geneva Conference of 1954 brought Ho Chi Minh another bitter experience with western negotiators. He had liberated Vietnam, and now had to surrender half of it, at least temporarily. Perhaps the North Vietnamese never really believed that an election would be held in 1956, even though —as President Eisenhower himself said—Ho Chi Minh's popularity throughout his nation, North and South, ensured him of 80 per cent of the southern vote. In any case, the United States again supported the enemies of Ho Chi Minh, this time the Diem regime of Saigon, which canceled the promised elections. Financially and militarily, the Diem regime could not stand without United States will and effort; it was no wild claim when Ho Chi Minh called it a puppet regime, and said that the United States had replaced the

[8] In *Commentary*, May, 1966.
[9] In *The Bitter Heritage* (Boston: Houghton Mifflin, 1967).

French as a foreign controlling power in the destiny of Vietnam.

But the whole context of Southeast Asia must also be taken into account. As early as 1949, the Chinese Communists had called a conference in Peking to announce the strategy of "wars of liberation." This strategy had proved successful in their case (in China, too, the United States had been the clearly denominated foreign enemy). No other national group found itself in so classic a Chinese situation as the Vietnamese delegation: they already had (1) a national front in which the Communists were the dominant force, (2) a national army, and (3) an immensely popular leader. Besides, their colonial masters, the French, were particularly vulnerable, since their control extended only to the population of the cities, whereas the vastly more populous rural areas were seriously disaffected. The Communist pledge of land reform spoke directly to the needs of the rural population, and (after 1959) guerrilla cadres were conscripted easily and instilled with high dedication and excellent morale. Moreover, the Communist party of Vietnam was unified with the Communist party of Laos, Cambodia, and Thailand. Ho Chi Minh wrote ambitiously of a united Southeast Asia. Only in 1959 did the Vietnamese Communists, in deference to nationalistic ambitions in other nations, declare these various parties to be independent. At the Geneva Conference in 1954, for example, the North Vietnamese delegate had signed for the Pathet Lao and the Khmer Resistance Forces. Legalistic distinctions, in short, are not easily made to hold up in the tracklessness of politics in Southeast Asia.[10]

How did the U.S. become involved in Vietnam? Richard N. Goodwin[11] thinks it was "almost by accident." Senator McGovern[12] has agreed. Arthur M. Schlesinger, Jr.,[13] makes almost the same point.[14] The United States intervention does

---

[10] See Benjamin Schwartz, "Chinese Visions and American Policies," *Commentary,* April, 1966; also Oscar Gass, "Vietnam —Resistance or Withdrawal?" *Commentary,* May, 1964.

[11] *Op. cit.*

[12] *Op. cit.*

[13] *Op. cit.*

[14] The documents collected by Marvin E. Gettleman in *Vietnam* (Greenwich: Fawcett, 1965) support this view.

not appear, in any case, to have been by design or according to policy. The roots of the U.S. commitment to the French after 1945 are obscure. The commitment to Diem after 1954, as President Eisenhower has made clear, did not involve the pledge of American armies in the field; Eisenhower assigned to Diem himself the task of fighting subversion. Neither the Geneva Accords nor the SEATO treaty (of which South Vietnam is not a signatory) binds the United States to such intervention. In fact, as Senators Morse and Gruening have often made clear on the floor of the Senate, the United States intervention in South Vietnam is *prohibited* by several provisions of the SEATO treaty and by provisions of the charter of the United Nations. Slowly, reluctantly, by the commitment first of military advisers (after all, North Vietnamese cadres were being trained in China) and then of Green Berets and other agents (who penetrated into North Vietman as well as into the mountain areas of South Vietnam), the United States pledged itself in actions even if not in words to involvement in the affairs of South Vietnam.

The most concise and trenchant account of this involvement has been presented by Theodore Draper.[15] Full documentation is given. Mr. Draper divides the U.S. involvement into five stages, and in what follows I have followed his account closely, expanding it at points from other sources. The general progress is from political failure to military escalation. At every step, American political acumen has been defective and American political performance maladroit. Then, rather than admit failure or take the political steps to amend it, Americans have called for further military violence—as if our nation knew nothing better than how to throw heavy armaments around. The picture (it is not Draper's alone) is sad: Americans appear in the role of clumsy wielders of destruction, men made afraid by their own fantasies, men who act violently and then invent reasons afterwards, men caught up in countless lies in order to justify the process. Surely religious men will agree that the only cure for past mistakes is humble confession and amendment; the bitter truth about our recent conduct must be faced.

[15] "The American Crisis," *Commentary*, January, 1967.

The First Stages

In 1954, President Eisenhower declared that he "could conceive of no greater tragedy than for the United States to become involved in an all-out war in Indochina." Nine years later, in September, 1963, President Kennedy said: "In the final analysis, it is their war. They are the ones to win it or lose it. We can help them, we can give them equipment, we can send our men out there as advisers, but they have to win it—the people of Vietnam—against the Communists." The next year, in March, 1964, Secretary of Defense McNamara said: "The large indigenous support that the Vietcong receives means that solutions must be as political and economic as military. Indeed, there can be no such thing as a purely 'military' solution to the war in South Vietnam." During the election campaign of 1964, even President Johnson was saying: "We don't want to get tied down in a land war in Asia. . . . We are not about to send American boys nine or ten thousand miles away from home to do what Asian boys should be doing for themselves."

The first stage in the United States military intervention in Vietnam was the enormous financial assistance given to the French; but the second stage was the choice of Ngo Dinh Diem as the man on whom to stake the United States policy after the French defeat. Diem did not take part in the struggle for national independence; he spent his time making friends in Washington. Simultaneous with the beginning of Diem's term in office in 1954, John Foster Dulles requested that a team of army experts study the practicality of a large-scale United States intervention in Indochina now that the French were giving way. According to Lieutenant General James M. Gavin, the military study of 1954 predicted that eight infantry divisions and thirty-five engineer battalions would be needed for such an intervention.

In October, 1954, President Eisenhower wrote the famous letter which is one of the main texts by which supporters of the present intervention demonstrate a U.S. "commitment" to South Vietnam. In this letter, Eisenhower promised aid to Diem, "provided that your government is prepared to give assurances as to the standards of performance it would be able to maintain in the event such aid were supplied." Eisenhower hoped that American aid would make the government of Vietnam "a strong viable state, capable of resisting attempted subversion or aggression through military means." Ten years later, President Johnson was to say: "Our commitment today is just the same as the commitment made by President Eisenhower in 1954." The only difference was that President Eisenhower had laid the burden of "resisting attempted subversion or aggression" on the government of Vietnam.

Diem established a vigorous and cruel dictatorship in Saigon. From 1954 until 1957, his rude and violent methods proved amazingly successful. He temporarily broke up the strength of three sects and their armies and established a unified regime. He took the initiative from the few Communists, treating them like many other of his enemies, attacking them before they had provoked it. (Hanoi's leaders were facing an internal revolt in North Vietnam.) So effective was Diem's campaign against the Communists that he almost broke the party's morale, and defections were numerous. The State Department's White Paper of 1965 reports that after Diem's attacks Communist cadres had to be "rebuilt, reorganized and expanded." It also makes clear that the Communists had begun with a strategy that stopped "short of open violence." Nationalist terrorism began much later, in 1957-58, and the first "really military assaults" began in 1960 with an attack of 260 men (carrying 170 weapons) upon a government weapons depot.

The Communists were not Diem's only enemy. Draper writes: "By 1956, Diem was well on his way to creating a police state which silenced, exiled, imprisoned and put to death all rivals and critics indiscriminately. His repression atomized and pulverized the Vietnamese society which he had just succeeded in giving some semblance of unity. The Communists picked up allies as quickly as he made enemies." From 1957 on, the Diem regime was destroying itself.

Ambassador Frederick E. Nolting, Jr., was told in April, 1961, before he left for his new post in Saigon that "it would be a miracle if South Vietnam lasted three months longer." The threat to South Vietnam did not come from the Communists but from the Diem regime. Bernard Fall estimates guerrilla strength in 1959 at three thousand, and the White Paper of February, 1965, which, if anything, exaggerates

Communist strength, estimates that only 1,800 to 2,700 men were infiltrated from the North in 1959-60. Diem had cut himself off from almost every other faction in Vietnamese life but his own. The nation was decaying from within; the United States public has never been told how deeply that decay has struck.

The next stage in the United States involvement was initiated by President Kennedy in 1961, when Diem had been in power seven years. On the political question of how to deal with Diem, Kennedy succumbed to fatalism. He disliked the situation he had inherited, but went along with it. Then he added to his troubles by sending to Saigon a new ambassador, Frederick E. Nolting, Jr., and a new military commander, General Paul Harkins, who were of a mind to give enthusiastic support to Diem. Their enthusiasm mired the United States more deeply in a trap. Kennedy's second decision was to reject the extant plans for introducing American ground forces into the South and for bombing military targets in the North. But he did agree, in face of the bankrupt political situation, to make America's response primarily military. He increased the number of advisers from about 800 to about 17,000.

These two factors—fatalism in drifting with the past, and steady gravitation from political failure to military cover—are the two outstanding characteristics of the United States involvement in South Vietnam. They characterize the administrations of all three American Presidents, Eisenhower, Kennedy, and Johnson, in dealing with Vietnam.

Another turning point in the United States involvement was the assassination of Diem. It seems that the United States did not positively plan the downfall of Diem, but it certainly did not stand in the way. The Australian writer Denis Warner wrote that "the tyranny the West allied with in Saigon was in many ways worse than the tyranny it was fighting against." [16] Diem and his family had murdered or exiled all potential opposition; his passing left a vacuum in South Vietnamese leadership. Diem had "lost the confidence and loyalty of his people," as Secretary McNamara put it on March 26, 1964.

During the next year, one general after another was to try his hand at governing South Vietnam. The United States

[16] *The Last Confucian* (Baltimore: Penguin, 1964).

still tried to interpret the war in political and economic, as well as military terms. In August, 1964, the State and Defense Departments published *Vietnam: The Struggle for Freedom.*[17] This booklet argued against the use of American combat units in Vietnam, since they would be unequipped for fighting a guerrilla war. Besides, the pamphlet went on, the employment of American combat units would provide "ammunition for Communist propaganda which falsely proclaims that the United States is conducting a 'White man's war' against Asians." Six months later, the government of the United States would have made a decision to send two hundred thousand troops to Vietnam. What could have happened during this six months so to change the character of the war?

Afraid of Four Hundred Men

It seems incredible that the next turning point in the United States involvement was the moving of four hundred regular troops from North Vietnam in December of 1964. The official explanation of the massive use of American troops is that the North Vietnamese 325th Division moved into the South late in 1964. General William C. Westmoreland recently said: "Early in 1965 we knew that the enemy hoped to deliver the *coup de grâce* by launching a major summer offensive to cut the Republic of Vietnam in two with a drive across the central highlands to the sea. I had to make a decision, and did. I chose a rapid buildup of combat forces, in the full knowledge that we should not have a fully developed logistic base to support these forces." [18]

The South Vietnamese government and its army was so weak that it was ready to collapse. This collapse could hardly have been due solely to the pressures of the Vietcong, let alone to the pressures from the North Vietnamese. Bernard Fall wrote in October, 1965: "No Intelligence officer was ready to swear that the 325th as a unit had joined the battle in South Vietnam." [19] Thus, ten months after it was supposed to have infiltrated in the South, the 325th Division could not be found. The White Paper said that between 4,400 and

[17] (U.S. Government Printing Office, 1964).
[18] *U.S. News and World Report,* November 28, 1966.
[19] *The New Republic,* October 9, 1965.

7,400 North Vietnamese had entered the South in all of 1964; so in any case, it was a very small division. *Even a full year later,* at the end of 1965, a congressional committee led by Senator Mike Mansfield visited South Vietnam and reported that North Vietnamese regular soldiers made up only 14,000 of the supposed enemy force of 230,000 men. Then Mansfield later said in an address at Yeshiva University: "When the sharp increase in the American military effort began in early 1965, it was estimated that only about 400 North Vietnamese soldiers were among the enemy forces in the South, which totaled one hundred and forty thousand at that time." Correspondent Ted Knap received a confirmation of these figures from the Defense Department.[20]

In February, 1965, the United States began to bomb North Vietnam. By the end of the year, nearly 200,000 American troops had been brought ashore. The rationalization given was that these troops were in response to "foreign aggression." But even at their most generous, official estimates reported 14,000 North Vietnamese regular troops in the country; and the famous arrival of the 325th Division, which was said to have changed everything, numbered 400 men. The truth of the matter seems to be that the American support of Diem, and of the successors of Diem, was an almost total political misjudgment. Instead of admitting a political mistake, the United States was turning to what it knew best: military power.

Thus in 1965 the Americans needed a new theory about Vietnam. Before that date, the war was treated predominantly as a "civil war." From the time of the United States decision to commit large numbers of combat troops to Vietnam, the blame was placed upon "foreign aggression." A civil war required political and economic efforts; "foreign aggression" called for a frankly military response. The new language seems to have come as a great relief to those who had to defend American intervention. But by the same token, a predominantly military response to a basically political problem was bound to make things worse.

The bureau chief of *Newsweek* reported in September, 1966: "We have yet to convince even those Vietnamese dwelling in the most secure areas of the country that there

[20] *Washington Daily News,* June 23, 1966.

is a cause worth fighting for." The South Vietnamese, he wrote, "seem to be able to maintain an almost total impassivity . . . most Vietnamese appear to be so many Stoic islands, as immune to the war as they are to the monsoon rains." They seem to be "a people abnormally detached from the brutal reality" of the battlefields around them. There is a "callous unconcern" for the welfare of Vietnamese soldiers who "lack incentive to fight aggressively." Worse, "the greatest indifference to the war effort is found among Vietnam's young people." [21]

Mr. Draper argues that one root of this internal political malaise goes back to June, 1956, when Diem abolished the age-old system of village government.[22] Bernard Fall describes the local election system which existed before 1956 as "the real cradle of a Jeffersonian type of representative government in the country." Now, *Newsweek* reported, the Americans "have wasted all the years since the revolution against Diem by not fostering local democracy in areas that were secure. Instead, we have allowed the Vietnamese corps commanders and their subordinates to become entrenched as local warlords."

Similarly Neil Sheehan wrote in the *New York Times Magazine* in October, 1966, of "Mandarin families that held titles to properties they had no intention of renouncing," who "seek to retain what privilege they have and to regain those they have lost." [23] He added:

> In Vietnam, only the Communists represent revolution and social change, for better or worse according to a man's politics. The Communist party is the one truly national organization that permeates both North and South Vietnam. The men who lead the party today, Ho Chi Minh and the other members of the politburo in Hanoi, directed the struggle for independence from France and in the process captured much of the deeply felt nationalism of the Vietnamese people. Perhaps because of this, the Communists, despite their brutality and deceit, remain the only Vietnamese capable of rallying millions of their countrymen to sacrifice and hardship in the name of the nation

[21] *Newsweek*, September 12, 1966.
[22] *Op. cit.*
[23] *New York Times Magazine*, October 9, 1966.

and the only group not dependent on foreign bayonets for survival.[24]

> In December, 1966, Marvin L. Stone wrote in the conservative *U.S. News and World Report* that the government troops have "less effective presence in the villages now than there was three years ago." He found the corruption worse than it had been under Diem.

> Not only is government security lacking, but Saigon's land-reform program, so vital to the aspirations of peasants, has never really been put in motion. In the secure areas, tenant farmers—that means 70 per cent of all farmers in the Delta—still are forced to pay up to 50 per cent and more of their rice crops to absentee landlords who have no obligation in return. A law on the books since 1955 sets the limit at 25 per cent.[25]

America Takes Over

The next turning point in American policy occurred at the Manila Conference of October, 1966. The United States assumed responsibility for carrying out the aggressive military operations of the war. The number of United States troops was projected towards the half million mark. The South Vietnamese army would be used for "pacification." Once more the American government knew only one "reasonable response" to the problems of Vietnam: more military force. In November, Ambassador Henry Cabot Lodge reported that despite the large military buildup of 1966, five basic features of the problem in Vietnam had changed little or not at all. These were: the mileage of open roads, the percentage of population living in security, the percentage of population living under domination of the Vietcong, the daily number of victims to Communist terrorism, and the rate of Vietcong military recruitment.

Moreover, although the United States buildup in 1965 had prevented a complete collapse in South Vietnam, the strength of the opposition was now far greater than five

---

[24] *Ibid.*

[25] *U.S. News and World Report*, December 5, 1966.

years earlier. Mr. Lodge gave the following figures: North Vietnamese regulars "approximately 50,000"; southern military units "100,000"; and highly trained "guerrilla terrorist" units in the villages "150,000." Mr. Lodge described this third group as "the real cancer." It is obvious from his figures that even the defeat of the small number of North Vietnamese troops committed to the war would not measurably alter the basic situation.

One month later, Mr. Lodge added that the 150,000 terrorists in the villages could not be successfully dealt with "until we've rebuilt the whole political, social, and economic structure in this country."

In brief, the United States will have to turn South Vietnam into a virtual colony, remaking the entire country from top to bottom. The South Vietnamese no longer share in "the major fighting," for which it is obvious they have little heart. In order to "free" the country, and to "rebuild" it, the United States now applies more military pressure. But this pressure does not come from putting one million or perhaps two million American soldiers in the field—the number that would seem to be required to police every village in the country and so root out the 150,000 terrorists. It comes rather from heavier fire power: B-52's, tactical air, artillery, and armor.

A new stage in the war was reached at the end of February, 1967, when American artillery began shelling North Vietnam, American ships offshore began shelling North Vietnam, and mines were sown in rivers in North Vietnam. The United States was not—unless secretly—sending men across the borders into North Vietnam. But in every other way at her disposal, by sea and by air, the United States was invading North Vietnam. The official reason for the enlargement of the war was now "to make the other side realize the high cost of this war and to make it too expensive to continue." But even if the United States destroyed all the industrial capacity of North Vietnam, this destruction would set that country back at most to 1945. The basic life and strength of North Vietnam would hardly have been changed. The United States would have shown how powerful its technology is. It would not have shown a great deal of political skill, human sensitivity, or common sense.

Inheriting a Moral Nightmare

Americans have a tradition of giving the benefit of the doubt to their leaders. Americans think of themselves and of their leaders as basically decent and humanitarian. Consequently, it is almost impossible for them to admit the truth about what is happening in Vietnam. The truth is too terrible.

Yet if we agree that Presidents Eisenhower, Kennedy, and Johnson have acted in good faith, how are we to explain the moral degradation in which we have become involved? The Secretary General of the United Nations, U Thant, was driven by his observations to call this mismatch between United States technology and a small underdeveloped nation one of the "most barbarous" wars in history.

Nothing makes the barbarity plainer than the letters from soldiers in the field collected in *Letters From Vietnam.*[20] ". . . the Vietcong aren't the only ruthless ones," a sailor writes. "*We* have to be, too. *Have* to. You'd be surprised to know that a guy you went to school with is right now shooting a nine-year-old girl and her mother. Or throwing a Vietcong out of a helicopter because he wouldn't talk." Another writes:

> The going here is pretty rough, and all the dirty fighting isn't on one side. A week ago our platoon leader brought in three prisoners. . . . This guy from Intelligence had all three lined up. One was a woman. He stripped her down to the waist and stripped the two men all the way. He had a little gadget I thought was a walkie-talkie or something. He stuck one end of this wire to the lady's chest and it was a kind of electric shock, because she got a real bad burn. From what she was screaming, my buddy and I could figure she didn't know anything.
>
> Then they took this same wire and tried it on the lady's husband and brother, but on their lower parts. I grabbed the damn thing and stuck it to the backass of the guy from Intelligence.
>
> Ever since that day I've been sick to my stomach and haven't been out on patrol or anything. My sergeant tells

[20] Glenn Munson, ed., *Letters From Vietnam* (New York: Parallax Publishing Co. and Pocket Books, 1966). Retail price, $1; quoted by permission.

me I'm suffering from battle fatigue and might get sent home.

We wish we could send you a couple of those electrical gadgets to use on the powers that sent and keep us here. This must end soon or a lot of us will go nuts.

Another writes:

In fighting over here I have seen things done that I know are war crimes; they say this is all right, because our men are getting killed by the Vietcong. But there still is a right and wrong—there has to be, or we will become no more than outright killers ourselves.

I have seen people killed that had their hands in the air. I have seen a man killed that was already hurt and had no weapons; the sergeant just cut his head off. Also a lot of people here are carrying around ears of people. The policy here is anyone killed is a Vietcong, so (they don't) care who you are if by chance you get shot; they say "He was a Vietcong." I have heard officers say that to their men.

Well, that is all I have to say on the matter as of now. They have been getting on me already for writing my Senator, and they know how I feel about what is going on that the people back home don't know.

Another writes to "Marilyn":

Before I start this letter, I want you to promise to forget it, as soon as you've read it—but I've got to talk to *someone*. Maybe, if I write about it, I'll be able to understand it a little more. . . .

Yesterday I shot and killed a little 8- or 9-year-old girl, with the sweetest, most innocent little face, and nastiest grenade in her hand, that you ever saw.

Myself and six others were walking along, when she ran out to throw that grenade at us. Of course there is always the old argument that it was us or her, but *what* in hell right did I have to kill a little child? All I can do is ask God to forgive me—I can't forgive myself.

This damned war seems so senseless at times; I can kill a man, and it doesn't bother me any more, but to kill a sweet little baby, who hasn't even learned right from wrong yet! *No* man has that right, or duty, or anything else you want to call it.

I'll be leaving here before too long, but to the last day of my life, I'll never be able to justify that. I really wonder what kind of man, or should I say animal, I've become. I know God will forgive me, but *I* have to live with myself.

I guess this isn't the kind of letter that you'd expect from a tough, hard Marine sergeant—but even we have feelings yet. Please, don't misunderstand: Right now I'm bitter, hurt, and so damned twisted up inside that I don't know what to think any more. Just bear with me, and one of these days I'll be back to myself, at least I sure hope so.

One of the things that I've always believed in was children. I love all kids. But how can I ever say that again?

I guess I've said enough for now. Thanks for "listening."

All war is barbarous; one cannot be squeamish. The special quality of this war, however, is that it is a war without front lines, a war without armies in uniform. Most of the enemy forces are mixed in with the civilian population. Correspondents like Neil Sheehan have reported from the field that far more civilians are killed than soldiers or terrorists. The lowest estimate of the ratio of civilian to military deaths is 3-1; not the highest by half is 9-1. Some soldiers in the field report that they have *seen* the cruelty of communism in operation, and they think of themselves as fighting to protect freedom and decency. But what do Vietnamese civilians think about the American cruelty which they have seen? For the cruelest part of the American operation is that it employs such vast and impersonal fire power. To be sure, an American army has never fought with so many political restrictions being placed upon it. And the explanation given for the immense fire power is that it "saves American lives." But an unasked question lurks beneath this explanation. Are American lives worth more than Vietnamese lives? Does one "rebuild" a country by pounding it with bombs, defoliating it, razing its villages, scarring its people with napalm (most gruesome of all U.S. weapons)? It now appears that far more civilians are killed by U.S. bombing than by Communist terror. The United States may have good intentions. But the moral dilemma is that in carrying them out we seem involved in greater evils than we dare to admit, evils which seem as great as those we oppose. We have become like our enemies.

Another way of stating the moral dilemma of the United States is that it wishes to intervene on the side of South Vietnam—for reasons that are constantly shifting their ground—but *to pay the lowest political cost possible.* In order to maintain popular support at home, American policy must have as its guideline a minimal loss of American life. The war in Vietnam is not popular; the American people would not tolerate lengthy casualty lists. Consequently, the American government cannot send a proper number of soldiers into the field; a million, perhaps two million, men would be required to ferret the guerrillas out rifle by rifle. Instead, the United States is relying upon enormously heavy fire power. The United States is taking the cheapest course possible. American lives will be saved. The South Vietnamese people and countryside must pay the costs.

The political consequences of this immense destruction are not now discernible. What kind of life will be possible in Vietnam after the war? How many displaced persons, broken families, razed villages, destroyed schools, and mutilated farm lands can an underdeveloped rural country support? And how, in the future generations, will Americans be remembered? What will other nations in Asia think about before asking the United States to come to their assistance?

Except for one matter, the burden of proof in this wasteful war lies upon those who support the American intervention in Vietnam. That one matter is that the United States, for better or worse, already *is* in Vietnam. The United States intervention cannot be wished away. It stands there as a rock of fact. The problem is how to get the United States *out* of South Vietnam, with more good than harm.

By now, many thousand American soldiers have been killed in Vietnam and tens of thousands maimed. Their comrades-in-arms and families will wish their lives not to have been spent in vain. It is politically necessary for the United States to show some worthy fruits from this bloody operation: a free election (even if the election goes Communist), a return to some sort of normalcy, a decent peace and prosperity in the next decade of Vietnam's bitter history.

But the United States will also have to clarify its national interest in Southeast Asia. Must a base at Camranh Bay be maintained in perpetuity as a check against Chinese expansion, like another Guantanamo Bay? Can we tolerate a Communist regime in North Vietnam and perhaps, within the next ten years, a Communist government achieved by a free national election in South Vietnam too—a Vietnam ultimately united under Ho Chi Minh or his successor? Premier Ky and nearly every member of his cabinet are North Vietnamese; the rulers of Vietnam in the future are probably going to be from the North and, if the people are left to themselves, Communist. For by reports from all sides one sees that the strongest dynamic political force in Vietnam, identified with the thirty-year struggle for national independence, is the Communist party. And if we cannot tolerate such a situation, what are we going to do? Richard N. Goodwin has written of

> Our Alice-in-Wonderland situation in Vietnam. Rhetorically, almost everyone is beginning to agree with everyone else in opposing withdrawal, in doubting that we can win, and in wanting an intermediate position—and all the while the war steadily escalates. My own feeling is that it's going to escalate further. Yet no military expert has demonstrated that victory is possible short of completely obliterating that piece of the peninsula from the earth's surface.[27]

At least we can learn the following lessons from what we have done so far: (1) Military power is no substitute for political wisdom. (2) If it is communism we are supposed to be fighting, we have become as bad as we think Communists are. (3) If it is China we are supposedly fighting, we are foolish beyond words to be enmeshed in a land war on the Indochina peninsula. (4) If it is a civil war in Vietnam that we have entered into, the issue is one for the Vietnamese of North and South to settle among themselves; we cannot run their country for them.

---

[27] *Op. cit.*

No matter how one looks at it, we have made a staggering series of mistakes. We will not wipe out our mistakes by obliterating Vietnam.

Why We Have Done It

We are now in Vietnam. All fruitful discussion must begin with that fact. But if we clarify in our minds *why* we are there, perhaps we can find some way of extricating ourselves. When he was asked directly whether the explanation for the United States involvement might not be irrational rather than rational, Senator George McGovern had to agree: "The United States blundered into a war and needed a justification for it afterwards." [28] The Senator estimated that "perhaps ninety out of one hundred Senators think that we made a mistake in ever becoming involved in the first place."

Richard N. Goodwin elaborated:

> I don't think we went into Vietnam because of China. I think we got into Vietnam almost by accident. A commitment grew because at every stage we were under the illusion that we could buy a very cheap and easy victory there. In fact, I doubt if you will find China mentioned in the statements of any American President on Vietnam until the last six or eight months. It was a forbidden word. . . . At the present level of commitment, China proves to be the only rational reason for our presence there at all. Whether or not it *is* a rational reason, there is no doubt that the Chinese are much more aggressive in Vietnam today than they were, the Russians are much more aggressive in Vietnam than they were, and we are much more aggressive, because the issue has begun—very unfortunately, I believe—to transcend Vietnam itself. It has become a testing-ground of American power and will in that country and that part of the world. But I don't think this was at all the initial impulse that brought us there.[29]

Why, then, is the United States involved in Vietnam? Senator McGovern[30] asked officials at the highest levels of

[28] *Op. cit.*
[29] *Op. cit.*
[30] *Op. cit.*

our government and received two different answers. One was that our primary purpose was to stop a *Communist* takeover, even if its source were merely Hanoi. Another said there was no question but that if it weren't for *China* we would not be involved in Vietnam at all: we must hold the line against China's promotion of "wars of liberation" in Vietnam, or else hold that same line later in Laos, Thailand, Cambodia, and elsewhere in order to prevent the confrontation from becoming World War III. Now these answers imply two different kinds of policy. One is almost theological in tone; it is war against an alien ideology. The other is a matter of "power politics"; it is a war to stop nationalistic expansion on the part of China. The fact that the United States is investing millions of dollars in enormous permanent bases like those at Camranh Bay seems to show that the long-term checking of China, and certainly not a mere temporary intervention in Vietnam, is now figuring in the policies of American leaders.

In brief, it seems that Vietnam has, at the very least, become the pawn of cold war politics, a test case, a showdown. It seems in many respects to have become, like Spain in 1936, the testing ground of the technology of the big powers. The battle is fought on the terrain of Vietnam. But the prize at stake is not merely Vietnam—neither Vietnamese independence nor Vietnamese prosperity. Vietnam has become the victim of a war between ideologies or vast national power centers: ". . . a darkling plain/ Where ignorant armies clash by night."

Many of those who now defend the U.S. effort in Vietnam are convinced that we should never have entered upon a land war in Asia, least of all in South Vietnam. But, they argue, policy cannot be made on "might-have-beens." Once involved, we must make the best of a bad situation. But what is the best? And what is the "bad situation"?

Vietnam is one nation. No fact is more important to fix in mind than that one. The military division along the 17th parallel is an artificial one, intended to be temporary; the Geneva Accords clearly stated that the "military demarcation line is provisional and should not in any way be interpreted as constituting a political or territorial boundary." The more dynamic part of the nation is the North; the South is the agricultural region. About twelve million of the

South's fifteen million citizens live in rural areas. They have reason to resent the absentee landlords, the remoteness, and the corruption of the Saigon government; they do not know by firsthand experience the forced collectivization of the lands in the North. Both the landlords in the South and the bureaucracy in the North are out to keep the land from the peasants. In the South, however, the Vietcong make promises of land reform which no one can match; and they have skillfully exploited selective terrorism in order to demonstrate their control of the countryside and to extend it. In the North a larger proportion of the money taken from the people is spent for the people; there is far less "conspicuous consumption" than occurs among the luxury-loving mandarin families of the South. On the other hand, in the North, under the influence of Maoist principles, the Vietminh did not scruple after independence to put scores of thousands to death on the grounds that, in class war, the sins of fathers must be visited also upon their sons and that resistance to land reform must be ruthlessly crushed.

In the war against the Communists in Greece in 1948, the United States was extremely careful to respect the borders of neighboring Yugoslavia, neither bombing the territory of Yugoslavia nor sending agents into it. It was felt then that such pressures would have forced Yugoslavia to seek aid from Soviet Russia. In Vietnam by contrast—even though Yugoslavia supplied much more aid to Greece than North Vietnam to South Vietnam—the United States began bombing and infiltrating North Vietnam in early 1964, making North Vietnam increasingly beholden to China and Russia.

Consequently, the least the American people can do is ask our government to decide *which* of the three following motives now lies behind American policy in Vietnam. Granted that we are in South Vietnam; why are we *staying* there?

(1) Is it to prevent at any cost the establishment of a *Communist* regime? For example, through an election which would reunite North and South Vietnam? (Eleven years ago, in 1956, the United States supported Diem in canceling the election called for under the Geneva Accords when, according to President Eisenhower, Ho Chi Minh would have won 80 per cent of the votes.)

(2) Is it to block nationalistic expansion on the part of *China,* or to block the Chinese strategy of "wars of liberation" (a strategy known to Ho Chi Minh at least as early as it was known to Mao Tse-tung)?

(3) Is it to give the *South Vietnamese* a separate political identity, independent from the northern half of the nation, and then to allow the South Vietnamese to choose any form of government they wish, even a Communist government?

In brief, the three underlying issues—the cold war struggle against communism, the role of China, and the civil war in Vietnam—must be clearly sorted out. Do we stay in Vietnam for the sake of the South Vietnamese? In opposition to China? In opposition to communism under any guise?

It seems plain (though some may disagree) that the last two reasons for staying in South Vietnam are mistaken and irresponsible. The possibility must be faced by all, however, that—given the immense suffering of the Vietnamese as pawns in such a game—to stay for the last two reasons is immoral. But if the reason why we remain in Vietnam is for the sake of the South Vietnamese, then it seems quite clear that they themselves have more than enough troops (600,000) to overcome "aggression" from their fellow Vietnamese from the North (40,000). As for the South Vietnamese guerrillas in their midst, it seems equally obvious (1) that to obliterate the nation in the process of weeding out huge forces of internal opposition is madness, and (2) that the South Vietnamese must settle their own civil war, and may the stronger party win. If it is true that the South Vietnamese are war-weary and simply wish to be let alone, let us leave them alone. Let those who wish to resist fight their own battles. The United States cannot play God.

Of course, once a great nation has committed itself to a course of action, it must act with a certain firmness and consistency or else give rise to uncertainties and miscalculations on the part of other powers. Once one has taken up a task, one must carry it through to some reasonable point. But surely that point has been reached in South Vietnam.

No other world power is capable of moving 400,000 men a distance of ten thousand miles and supporting them with unparalleled efficiency. The United States has proved that it is not a "paper tiger." Neither Russia nor China has been able to enter the struggle in any comparable way. They have tried to do through talk, bluster, and political action what we have done with brute force. Everyone in the world must know by now that the United States has the power to blast Vietnam from the face of the earth. Militarily, we have nothing left to prove to anybody—except perhaps to our own insecurities. Who could blame us if we said: "See here, we can destroy this tiny backward nation in seven days. But that would be senseless. Let everybody be warned that we can carry such a war to any quarter of the world, as no one else can. But in order not to bring about any more destruction, we are deescalating. The South Vietnamese now have a chance to negotiate the questions of national unity, a new form of government, and electoral procedures for themselves. Let them wind up the civil war on their own. We will (1) stop bombing; and (2) withdraw our troops over (say) the next twelve-month period"?

The premise of such a position is that North and South Vietnam are one nation. If the North is the stronger party, are we to stay in the South forever? Now that we have granted South Vietnam a breather, little more can plausibly be asked of us. It may well be the course of political wisdom to let some new regime—perhaps eventually that of Ho Chi Minh or his successors—inherit the problems of South Vietnam. In that case, any future failures would be, not ours, but theirs. Having experience in the quagmire of South Vietnamese officialdom, social structure, and economic practices, we may feel quite relieved to let someone else accept the headaches.

President Johnson, Vice President Humphrey, and Secretary of State Dean Rusk have met critics of the war with the avowal that they, too, are seeking peace, not peace at any price, but an *honorable* peace. No doubt, the United States cannot immediately and on the instant pick up and withdraw from South Vietnam. One cannot escape from one's mistakes quite so simply. But it is difficult to see what the word *honor* can mean in such a context. It seems that since the Second World War the United States has been wrong in its policies regarding South Vietnam at almost every point. We have now spent vastly more money to destroy that country than we did to help build it when it needed our aid in the beginning of its development. After every one of our mistakes, we seem to have been mesmerized by our own "honor." No doubt there is a point in foreign relations when one's past actions commit one to a line of conduct, and when one's credibility in foreign affairs is at stake. An arbitrary, erratic pattern of behavior heightens the possibilities of miscalculation in many other areas of the world. Richard N. Goodwin has pointed out[31] some of the good effects in many quarters of the world of the vigor of the United States policy in Vietnam. It is heartening to think that some good may be derived from so much evil.

Nevertheless, it seems plain that the increasing and now almost total militarization of the war is brutal beyond all bounds. Consistency in a line of action that has progressively worse results is not a sign of sanity, let alone of wisdom. What will "an honorable peace" be worth two years from now, if the present pace of destruction is continued? How much can a small and almost primitive country absorb? It seems that in at least one respect the United States is learning an Oriental value, one which it used to mock: the United States is trying desperately to "save face."

The Values We Stand For

Many of us who love our country are sad to see its flag carried in *this* war. We might be as brave as anyone else in other wars, and as eager to leap to the defense of the values dear to our nation. But in regard to this war many have felt, from year to year, increasing shame. It was not in order that our flag might be carried in wars like this that men of the generations before us suffered and died for liberty, for bravery, for justice. Our flag was inspired by our own struggle for national independence. It was once our cry, too, that "United we stand, divided we fall." We, too, were once opposed to tyranny. We have said harsh things about other colonialists.

Albert Camus wrote: "I would like to be able to love justice and still love my country." It is not that we think our national leaders have been cruel, or venal, or vicious. But many of us believe that they have been unwilling to recognize mistakes, mistakes made in good faith, but mistakes nonetheless. They have been led by a kind of fatalism which has accepted each present situation as irretrievable,

[31] *Op. cit.*

and in every case they have responded to their mistakes by raising the level of military violence. It is this fatalism, and this constant turn to greater violence, that we deplore as contrary to the traditions of our own country. We do not ask for immediate and thoughtless withdrawal. But we do ask that the nation which has initiated each new escalation of violence initiate the procedures of deescalation, and as speedily as possible turn the nation of Vietnam—its internal dissensions, its long-suffering people—over to its own population.

There does not seem to be a single good reason why this war must go on, except the need of the Americans to find "an honorable peace." In international politics, such matters are no doubt important. But since all the world knows that the United States has the power to raze every tree in Vietnam if we wish to do so, it will hardly count against us if we decide not to destroy what we could so easily destroy. Every single day of destruction and bloodshed makes the future rebirth of the country so much more difficult and improbable. The course we have chosen, a course of total militarization, destroys everything: the landscape, the people, the hopes for the future, the possibilities of any but a craven capitulation from others, and all pride in ourselves. When one has chosen a wrong course, whether by accident or by lack of foresight or by inertia, the only remedy is to change one's course.

A great number of young Americans have died in Vietnam. They will not have died in vain if we now choose the path of honesty, humility, compassion, and magnanimity. The country they died for is big enough to admit its mistakes—if not publicly, at least to itself—and to take its stand for human life rather than death, for creativity rather than destruction, for the honor that comes from self-correction rather than the honor that comes from "saving face."

II. The Moral Outrage of Vietnam

by ABRAHAM J. HESCHEL

On January 31, 1967, clergymen and laymen concerned about Vietnam assembled in Washington, D.C. At the worship service, I offered the following meditation on the words of the prophet Ezekiel (34:25-31):

Ours is an assembly of shock, contrition, and dismay. Who would have believed that we life-loving Americans are capable of bringing death and destruction to so many innocent people? We are startled to discover how unmerciful, how beastly we ourselves can be.

So we implore Thee, our Father in heaven, help us to banish the beast from our hearts, the beast of cruelty, the beast of callousness.

Since the beginning of history evil has been going forth from nation to nation. The lords of the flocks issue proclamations, and the sheep of all nations indulge in devastations.

But who would have believed that our own nation at the height of its career as the leader of free nations, the hope for peace in the world, whose unprecedented greatness was achieved through "liberty and justice for all," should abdicate its wisdom, suppress its compassion and permit guns to become its symbols?

America's resources, moral and material, are immense. We have the means and know the ways of dispelling prejudice and lies, of overcoming poverty and disease. We have the capacity to lead the world in seeking to overcome international hostility.

Must napalm stand in the way of our power to aid and to inspire the world?

To be sure, just as we feel deeply the citizen's dilemma, we are equally sensitive to the dilemma confronting the leaders of our government. Our government seems to recognize the tragic error and futility of the escalation of our involvement but feels that we cannot extricate ourselves without public embarrassment of such dimension as to cause damage to America's prestige.

But the mire in which we flounder threatens us with an even greater danger. It is the dilemma of either losing face or losing our soul.

At this hour Vietnam is our most urgent, our most disturbing religious problem, a challenge to the whole nation as well as a challenge to every one of us an individual.

When a person is sick, in danger or in misery, all religious duties recede, all rituals are suspended, except one: to save life and relieve pain.

Vietnam is a personal problem. To speak about God and remain silent on Vietnam is blasphemous.

> When you spread forth your hands
> I will hide my eyes from you;
> Yea when you make many prayers,
> I will not hear—
> Your hands are not clean.

In the sight of so many thousands of civilians and soldiers slain, injured, crippled, of bodies emaciated, of forests destroyed by fire, God confronts us with this question:

Where art thou?

Is there no compassion in the world? No sense of discernment to realize that this is a war that refutes any conceivable justification of war?

The sword is the pride of man; arsenals, military bases, nuclear weapons lend supremacy to nations. War is the climax of ingenuity, the object of supreme dedication.

Men slaughtering each other, cities battered into ruins: such insanity has plunged many nations into an abyss of disgrace. Will America, the promise of peace to the world, fail to uphold its magnificent destiny?

The most basic way in which all men may be divided is between those who believe that war is unnecessary and those who believe that war is inevitable; between those to whom the sword is the symbol of honor and those to whom seeking to convert swords into plowshares is the only way to keep our civilization from disaster.

Most of us prefer to disregard the dreadful deeds we do over there. The atrocities committed in our name are too horrible to be credible. It is beyond our power to react vividly to the ongoing nightmare, day after day, night after night. So we bear graciously other people's suffering.

O Lord, we confess our sins, we are ashamed of the inadequacy of our anguish, of how faint and slight is our mercy. We are a generation that has lost the capacity for outrage.

We must continue to remind ourselves that in a free society, all are involved in what some are doing. *Some are guilty, all are responsible.*

Prayer is our greatest privilege. To pray is to stake our very existence, our right to live, on the truth and on the supreme importance of that which we pray for. Prayer, then, is radical commitment, a dangerous involvement in the life of God.

In such awareness we pray . . .

We do not stand alone. Millions of Americans, millions of people all over the world are with us.

At this moment praying for peace in Vietnam we are spiritually Vietnamese. Their agony is our affliction, their hope is our commitment.

God is present wherever men are afflicted.

Where is God present now?

We do not know how to cry, we do not know how to pray!

Our conscience is so timid, our words so faint, our mercy so feeble.

O Father, have mercy upon us.

Our God, add our cries uttered here to the cries of the bereaved, crippled, and dying over there.

Have mercy upon all of us.

Help us to overcome the arrogance of power. Guide and inspire the President of the United States in finding a speedy, generous, and peaceful end to the war in Vietnam.

The intensity of the agony is high, the hour is late, the outrage may reach a stage where repentance will be too late, repair beyond any nation's power.

We call for a covenant of peace, for reconciliation of America and all of Vietnam. To paraphrase the words of the prophet Isaiah (62:1):

> For Vietnam's sake I will not keep silent,
> For America's sake I will not rest,
> Until the vindication of humanity goes forth as brightness,
> And peace for all men is a burning torch.

Here is the experience of a child of seven who was reading in school the chapter which tells of the sacrifice of Isaac:

> Isaac was on the way to Mount Moriah with his father; then he lay on the altar, bound, waiting to be sacrificed. My heart began to beat even faster; it actually sobbed with pity for Isaac. Behold, Abraham now lifted the knife. And now my heart froze within me with fright. Suddenly, the voice of the angel was heard: "Abraham, lay not thine hand upon the lad, for now I know that thou fearest God." And here I broke out in tears and wept aloud. "Why are you crying?" asked the Rabbi. "You know that Isaac was not killed."

> And I said to him, still weeping, "But, Rabbi, supposing the angel had come a second too late?"
> The Rabbi comforted me and calmed me by telling me that an angel cannot come late.

An angel cannot be late, but man, made of flesh and blood, may be.

■ ■ ■

Military Victory—A Moral Defeat

It is weird to wake up one morning and find that we have been placed in an insane asylum. It is even more weird to wake up and find that we have been involved in slaughter and destruction without knowing it.

What is being done by our government is done in our name. Our labor, our wealth, our civic power, our tacit consent are invested in the production and use of the napalm, the bombs, and the mines that explode and bring carnage and ruin to Vietnam.

The thought that I live a life of peace and nonviolence turns out to be an illusion. I have been decent in tiny matters on a tiny scale, but have become vicious on a large scale. In my own eyes my existence appears to be upright, but in the eyes of my victims my very being is a nightmare.

A sense of moral integrity, the equation of America with the pursuit of justice and peace, has long been part of our self-understanding. Indeed, for generations the image of America has been associated with the defense of human rights and the hope for world peace. And now history is sneering at us.

A ghastly darkness has set in over our souls. Will there be an end to dismay, an end to agony?

The encounter of man and God is an encounter within the world. We meet within a situation of shared suffering, of shared responsibility.

This is implied in believing in One God in whose eyes there is no dichotomy of here and there, of me and them. They and I are one; here is there, and there is here. What goes on over there happens even here. Oceans divide us, God's presence unites us, and God is present wherever man is afflicted, and all of humanity is embroiled in every agony wherever it may be.

Though not a native of Vietnam, ignorant of its language and traditions, I am involved in the plight of the Vietnamese. To be human means not to be immune to other people's suffering. People in Vietnam, North and South, have suffered, and all of us are hurt.

Unprepared, perplexed, uninformed, ill-advised, our nation finds herself in a spiritual inferno. Where do we stand? Where do we go from here? For a long time we suppressed anxiety, evaded responsibility. Yet the rivers of tears and blood may turn into a flood of guilt, which no excuse will stem.

The blood we shed in Vietnam makes a mockery of all our proclamations, dedications, celebrations. We have been moving from obscurity to confusion, from ignorance to obfuscation. Many are unaware, some acquiesce, most of us detest this unfathomable war, but are unable to envisage a way of getting out of this maze. Millions of Americans who cannot close their minds to the suffering and sorrow are stricken with anguish, and form a large fellowship living in a state of consternation.

We are killing the Vietnamese because we are suspicious of the Chinese. The aim is to kill the elusive Vietcong, yet to come upon one soldier, it is necessary to put an end to a whole village, to the lives of civilians, men, women, and children.

Is it not true that Communists are fellow human beings first, antagonists second? Politically, the concept of the enemy is becoming obsolete; yesterday's enemy is today's ally. The state of cold war between the United States and Soviet Russia has given place to a quest of friendly understanding.

The absurdity of this war is tacitly admitted by almost everyone. Our presence in Vietnam has become a national nightmare, our actions are forced, we dislike what we do; we do what we hate to do. Is this a way to bring democracy to Vietnam: more explosives, more devastation, more human beings crippled, orphaned, killed? Is it not clear that military victory in Vietnam would be a tragic moral defeat? That military triumph would be a human disaster?

The choice is clear. We decide either in favor of further escalation that may lead to a world war or in favor of gradual disengagement followed by negotiation. Refusal to embark upon a course of unlimited massacre will redound only to the honor of America. Did not the retreat of France from Algeria, where her involvement was incomparably more important, add to the glory of France? Did President Kennedy's self-restraint during the ill-planned expedition to the Bay of Pigs tarnish in any way the prestige of America?

Is it not the avowed policy of the United States to insist that there is an alternative to war?

We are fully aware of America's moral commitment to give aid to democratic governments all over the world when they are threatened or attacked by tyrants and dictators. However, we do not fight in Vietnam as allies of a freely elected democratic government but rather as fellow-travelers of anti-Communists, as allies of a despotic military oligarchy. Is it the destiny of our youth to serve as mercenaries in the service of military juntas all over the world?

Our major blunder is the fact that our aid and involvement is a government-to-government operation. Driven by our tendency to suspect social change, by our tendency to measure other peoples' values by our own standards, we have no communication with the people of Vietnam, nor have we sought to relate ourselves to their political understanding. We are in touch with military dictatorship, we ignore the people. We see the power structure, we disregard human beings.

We do not listen to their voice, we are ignorant of their way of thinking, traditions and scale of values. Our failure to convince the Vietnamese that our aim is to save their freedom, to insure their welfare, is not necessarily a sign of their being imbeciles.

Vietnam is a country which has for many decades been the victim of colonial demoralization. Injustice, poverty, exploitation prevail. Revolutionary change is a moral necessity.

Because the government of South Vietnam is corrupt, distrusted by and alienated from the majority of the people, our aid fails to reach the peasants. We are being misguided in maintaining that social revolution can be stopped by military operations. America's identification with Vietnamese juntas not only thwarts any effort to bring aid to the destitute peasants but defames our image in their eyes.

Can an outside power succeed in bringing a recalcitrant heretic community such as the National Liberation Front back to the fold by fire and sword? A major stumbling block to these efforts is our opponents' distrust in our desire for peace. Yet the atmosphere on both sides is infected with suspicion. The Golden Rule seems to be "suspect thy neighbor as thyself."

Indeed, how can there be trust in our desire for peace, if the call for negotiation is consistently followed by further escalation? The groan deepens, the combat burns, the wailing cry does not abate. Every act of escalation has as its effect further aggravation.

For on horror's head horrors accumulate. We are in danger of being swept away—against our will, despite circumspection—by a vehement current and compulsive course which never feels the retiring ebb but keeps on, due to a more violent pace, to an even wider torrent.

War tends to become its own end. Force unleashed moves on its own momentum, breaks all constraint, reaching intensities which man can no longer control. The nation's confidence both in the candor of the Administration and in the policy which it is pursuing in Vietnam is faltering, while the world's respect for American democracy has been profoundly shaken. America's image is tragically distorted.

For many years the world's eyes were directed to Washington, trusting that the White House, the spirit of America, would secure peace. Should the world's eyes be directed to Moscow, hoping that the Kremlin may use its influence to bring about peace in Vietnam?

What is it that may save us, that may unite men all over the world? The abhorrence of atrocity, the refusal of the conscience to accommodate to the arrogance of military power. Indeed, it is the power of the human conscience which has in the last twenty years inhibited the use of thermonuclear weapons. Yet the power of the conscience is tenuous and exceedingly vulnerable. Its status is undergoing profound upheavals. We are challenged too frequently, too radically to be able to react adequately.

However, the surrender of conscience destroys first the equilibrium of human existence and then existence itself. In the past, war was regarded as an instrument of politics. Today politics is in the process of becoming an instrument of military technology. How long can total war be avoided?

Militarism is whoredom, voluptuous and vicious, first disliked and then relished. To paraphrase the prophet's words "For the spirit of harlotry is within them, and they know not the Lord" (Hosea 5:4): "Samson with his strong body, had a weak head, or he would not have laid it in a harlot's lap."

Has Our Conscience Become a Fossil?

Has our conscience become a fossil? Is all mercy gone? If mercy, the mother of humanity, is still alive as a demand, how can we say Yes to our bringing agony to the tormented nation of Vietnam?

It is a war we can never win. For, indeed, our superior weapons may well destroy the cities and the hamlets, the fighting forces and the villagers who support them. However, what will our army have left behind? Tombs, tears, havoc, acrimony, and vast incentives to hatred and rage.

The world is not the same since Auschwitz and Hiroshima. The decisions we make, the values we teach must be pondered not only in the halls of learning but also in the presence of inmates in extermination camps, and in the sight of the mushroom of a nuclear explosion.

Those who pray tremble when they realize how staggering are the debts of the religions of the West. We have mortgaged our souls and borrowed so much grace, patience, and forgiveness. We have promised charity, love, guidance, and a way of redemption, and now we are challenged to keep the promise, to honor the pledge. How shall we prevent bankruptcy in the presence of God and man?

We have embarked on this adventure guided by the assumption that those who disagree with us are a threat to us; the assumption that what is good for America is good for Vietnam; that it is better to be dead than red; that communism is the only danger, the only evil which all must fight.

Must we proudly cling to our first mistake? Must Americans and Vietnamese die in order to honor a false decision?

Is War an Answer to Human Agony?

America has been enticed by her own might. There is nothing so vile as the arrogance of the military mind. Of all the plagues with which the world is cursed, of every ill, militarism is the worst: the assumption that war is an answer to human agony. There are many wild beasts in the human heart, but the beastliest of all is the brutality of arms.

No war remains within its limits; its road is not only downhill but steep. We have sown the wind, and we now reap the whirlwind.

The question addressed to every one of us personally and collectively is this: What shall I do to stop the killing and dying in Vietnam? It is this urgent question that we all have in common at this moment, challenging equally our integrity, our right to invoke the name of Him who is the Father of the Vietnamese as well as of the Americans. The war in Vietnam has plunged every one of us into unknown regions of responsibility. I am personally involved in the torment of the people injured in battle on the front and in the hamlets, in the shipping of explosives, in the triggering of guns. Though deaf to the distant cry of the orphaned and the maimed, I know that my own integrity is being slashed in that slaughter.

There is a deep and awesome power in blood that is spilled, in "the voice of the blood that cries from the earth." The voice of those who die in Vietnam abominates all of us.

The decision to use military force was a failure of statesmanship, a failure of nerve, a moral retreat. To deescalate now, people say, is difficult. What must not be forgotten is that to continue the war will make our situation even more difficult. Remember the price we pay when military pride is hurt. We have gone beyond the policy of brinkmanship. Are we prepared to descend into an abyss? War has ceased to be a human action, carried out with courage and volition. War today is an impersonal, mechanized process. It begins as darkness in the mind and creeps on as a spiritual pestilence, contaminating the power of decision.

There is abundance of weapons and scarcity of compassion. Arms are absolutes, reliable, infallible, while human understanding is relative, vacillating, open to question. So we put our trust in what the arms will do. It is not man any more who ascertains standards, directions. Vast military power tends to cultivate a sense of invincibility and to debilitate the delicate power of political and moral discernment. Decisions are made in terms of monstrosity. Statesmen surrender to the sovereignty of computers. The engine is driving the driver. Frankensteins are here.

Leading American authorities on international law maintain that the unilateral military intervention of the United States in Vietnam violates the charter of the United Nations; that the military presence of the United States in Vietnam violates the Geneva Accords of 1954; that the United States is not committed by the SEATO treaty or otherwise to intervene in Vietnam; that the intensity and destructiveness of United States warfare in Vietnam is contrary to international law; that the United States' actions in Vietnam violate treaties which are part of the supreme law of the land, and hence violate the United States Constitution.

Indeed, this is a war that cannot be waged within the terms of civilized rules of warfare. An advertisement in the *New York Times,* January 15, 1967, sponsored by a group of lawyers, said of the American campaign: "We, unintentionally, are killing and wounding three or four times more people than the Vietcong do. . . . We are not maniacs and monsters; but our planes range the sky all day and all night and our artillery is lavish, and we have much more deadly stuff to kill with. The people are there on the ground, sometimes destroyed by accident, sometimes destroyed because Vietcong are reported to be among them. This is indeed a new kind of war. . . ."

Where are the events leading to? Invasion of North Vietnam? Occupation of Laos and Cambodia? An encounter with the Chinese army?

The State Department and the Pentagon behave as if there were a division of qualities: infallibility of judgment in their possession; ignorance and sentimentality everywhere else.

Those of us who disagree with American policy on Vietnam are told by the State Department that since we do not possess all the facts, we are not competent to evaluate the situation. Yet some of us wonder whether the State Department alone has a monopoly on wisdom and vision. Is it not possible that the minds of those involved in a certain policy become addicted to it, and are hardly capable of undertaking an agonizing reappraisal that may prove how wrong the premises are?

There is a large community of concern for Vietnam which is also a community of concern about the inadequacy of our concern. In Vietnam people die, while we deliver speeches. In Vietnam people bleed, while all we do is send telegrams to Washington. We have succeeded in getting pictures of the moon, but have no picture of the agony of the Vietnamese, no picture of the spiritual agony of millions of Americans who are aghast at what is being done in their names.

The Crisis of Responsibility

Responsibility is the essence of being a person, the essence of being human, and many of us are agonized by a grave *crisis of responsibility.* Horrified by the atrocities of this war, we are also dismayed by the ineffectiveness of our protests, by the feebleness of our dissent. Have we done our utmost in expressing our anguish? Does our outcry match the outrage?

This is a unique hour in human history. It is within our might to decide whether this war is a prelude to doom, the beginning of the end, or whether to establish a precedent of solving a most complex crisis by abandoning slogans and clichés.

There is no alternative, we are told. Yet have we really exhausted all possibilities of negotiation? Is the state of humanity so overcome by insanity that all rationality is gone and war left as the only way? Is it really so simple? Are we Americans all innocent, righteous, full of saving grace, while our adversaries are all corrupt, wicked, insensitive to human rights?

Collision between states is not always due to a conflict of vital interests. It is often due to the tendency toward self-enhancement inherent in the monstrosity of power.

Worse than war is the belief in the inevitability of war. There is no such thing as inevitable war. And certainly the war in Vietnam was not inevitable. It came about as a failure of vision, as a result of political clichés, of thinking by analogies, of false comparisons, of blindness to the uniqueness of an extraordinary constellation. This war will not end by dropping bigger and better bombs, by an increase in ferocity, and by the merciless use of force. Vietnam is primarily a human problem, a human emergency, human anguish. There are no military solutions to human problems; violence and bloodshed are no answer to human anguish.

We feel alarmed by a policy that continues to be dogmatic, devoid of elasticity. The root of the tragedy is in the combination of global power and parochial philosophy, of most efficient weapons and pedestrian ideas. New thinking is called for; new contacts must be made. Leaders not directly involved in present operations must be consulted.

Let the American presence in Vietnam be a presence of understanding and compassion. America's war potential is great, but America's peace potential is even greater. Let there be an effort for friendship for Vietnam. Modern war is a mechanical operation. But peace is a personal effort, requiring deep commitment, hard, honest vision, wisdom and patience, facing one another as human beings, elasticity rather than dogmatism.

Would not sending a Peace Corps prove more helpful than sending more armed divisions?

We have entered an age in which military victories are tragic defeats, in which even small wars are exercises in immense disaster.

The public enemy number one is the nuclear bomb, the population explosion, starvation, and disease. It is the fear of nuclear war that unites men all over the world, East and West, North and South. It is fear that unites us today. Let us hope that the conquest of fear and the elimination of misery will unite us tomorrow.

This war, I am afraid, will not leave the nation where it found it. Its conclusion may be the beginning of a grave alienation. The speed and the spirit in which this war will end will fashion our own lives in the years that lie ahead.

On January 22, 1917, President Woodrow Wilson in his address to the Senate uttered a point of view which we pray President Lyndon Johnson would adopt as his own: "It must be a peace without victory." Let our goal be compromise, not victory.

In the name of our kinship of being human, the American people meet the Vietnamese face to face. Only few men are marble-hearted. And even marble can be pierced with patience and compassion. Let us create a climate of reconciliation. Reducing violence and tension, acts of goodwill are necessary prerequisites for negotiations. We must seek neither victory nor defeat. Our aim is to enable the South Vietnamese to find themselves as free and independent people.

The initiative for peace must come from the strong, out of a position of strength.

We will all have to strain our energies, crack our sinews, tax and exert our brains, cultivate understanding, open our hearts, and meet with all Vietnamese, North as well as South.

This is the demand of the hour: not to rest until—by excluding fallacies, stereotypes, prejudices, exaggerations which perpetual contention and the consequent hostilities breed—we succeed in reaching the people of Vietnam as brothers.

There is still time to unlearn old follies, there is still time to seek honest reconciliation. A few months from now it may be too late; a few months from now our folly may be beyond repair, sin beyond repentance.

It is not for man to decide who shall live and who shall die, who shall kill and who shall sigh. May no one win this war; may all sides win the right to live in peace.

III. An Appeal to the Churches and Synagogues

by ROBERT MCAFEE BROWN

Many people still question the right of the religious communities to take sides on political issues.

This is neither the time nor the place for an extended defense of the moral obligation of the religious communities to articulate their concern about Vietnam. All that will be done is to suggest, very briefly, four levels of involvement that seem appropriate to our present concern.

1. One task of the churches and synagogues is to *mediate and reconcile across chasms of misunderstanding and hostility.* This means maintaining lines of communication between nations in time of war; it also means providing a forum for the expression of differences of opinion *within* a nation. The churches and synagogues, believing that all men are made in God's image, must see to it that those with political differences continue to treat one another as human beings, capable of rational discourse, and must insist that the public debate avoid the level of name-calling or emotional argumentation devoid of facts.

But the danger of this position is that it will lead to blandness or neutrality, and that the churches and synagogues will be so concerned to act as impartial referees that they will fail to take sides on issues where morality demands taking sides. Vietnam has become such an issue.

2. It is the duty of churches and synagogues to *urge their members to speak and act responsibly in the political, social, and economic life of the nation.* Religion is not a private affair between the individual and God, but a cor-

porate affair between the individual, God, *and the neighbor.* It is the duty of the individual, both as religious person and as citizen, to play a responsible role in the processes of democracy—voicing his opinion, working for the election of public officials, voting, criticizing, supporting, challenging. The churches and synagogues must never let religion be used to permit individuals to escape such responsibility. There is no public issue concerning which this responsibility is greater than Vietnam.

3. The churches and synagogues must not only encourage individuals to speak out on public issues, but must take special pains to support them when such speaking involves *dissent* from government policy. The ultimate loyalty of Christian and Jew is not to government but to God. If and when ultimate loyalty to God compels dissent from government, the churches and synagogues must support the exercise of that ultimate loyalty. There is no time when the integrity of religious life or democratic procedures are in greater jeopardy than when the right of dissent is threatened. This is a principle of paramount importance, for the right of dissent is increasingly challenged in relation to our policy in Vietnam.

For many, the propriety of church and synagogue involvement stops with the encouragement of individual voices. Those who feel that it does, should at least support all efforts to mobilize such voices, and should seek to encourage every avenue of public opinion that will lead to reappraisal.

4. But a fourth type of involvement can be urged—the recognition that in addition to their responsibility to urge individuals to speak and act, churches and synagogues have *a responsibility to speak and act corporately.* It is not enough for the churches and synagogues to say to their members, "Go out into the public sector and behave in whatever way your conscience dictates." It is not even enough for them to give guidance in the formation of that individual conscience. For in the face of evil, corporate silence, when a corporate voice could have been heard and is not heard, becomes complicity with evil. A time comes when the issues are so momentous that not speaking at all is a greater sin even than speaking wrongly. For wrong speech can at least elicit right speech, whereas silence implies consent to an

evil that because of the silence escapes unchallenged. Consequently, those who are the leaders of the religious communities must speak in the name of their communities, both to their own members and through their own members to the nation and to the world, saying in effect, "Here is where our convictions inescapably lead us. In the name of our faith we cannot remain silent." (Examples of this corporate speaking by the World Council of Churches, the National Council of the Churches of Christ in the U.S.A., Pope Paul VI, the National Conference of Catholic Bishops, and the Synagogue Council of America, are contained in an Appendix to the present volume.)

None of this means that religious leaders can claim a political *expertise* denied to politicians, or that the political judgments of a denominational body are rendered accurate by prefacing them with the dangerous claim, "Thus saith the Lord." But it does mean that national policies can be questioned, political decisions challenged, and alternative courses of action proposed, in the name of concerns that sometimes escape the policymakers. Herbert Butterfield, the British historian, expresses the kind of perspective the policymakers often forget, but which the churches and synagogues must continue to intrude into the public debate, if his statement is not to become the epitaph of the American nation:

> The hardest strokes of heaven fall in history upon those who imagine that they can control things in a sovereign manner, as though they were kings of the earth, playing Providence not only for themselves but for the far future —reaching out into the future with the wrong kind of farsightedness, and gambling on a lot of risky calculations in which there must never be a single mistake.

Not only must individual Jews and Christians speak up; groups of Jews and Christians must also speak up. They must speak up so that the Administration will not be able to discount the voices of protest as the voices of mere individuals, but will be forced to face the fact of collective Protestant, Catholic, and Jewish outcry. If ever there was an "ecumenical" issue, i.e., an issue affecting the whole of the *oikoumene* (the inhabited world), it is Vietnam. In the face of the immensity of that issue, individual speech alone is frivolous if not immoral.

* * *

As we look back from some vantage point in the future at the increasing horror of the 1960's (always presuming that the horror will abate before it has destroyed us all), one question will have to haunt the churches and synagogues: "Where were you? As war was spreading, escalating, becoming more and more brutal, taking a heavier and heavier toll on civilian lives and international trust, *where was your voice?*"

History asks that question about the rise of Nazism in the 1930's in Germany, and notes the failure of the churches to speak up until it was too late. History asks that question about the battle for civil rights in the 1950's and 1960's in the United States, and notes the failure of the churches and synagogues to act until the eleventh hour. History will soon ask that question about a third great moral outrage of our era, Vietnam. Will the churches and synagogues maintain their silence, or will they finally realize that individual voices are not enough and that a great chorus of concern must be heard?

Before it is too late . . .

The Need to Speak

A time comes, therefore, when silence is betrayal. That time has long since come in relation to Vietnam. The fact that the word to be spoken is initially a word of judgment does not excuse the churches and synagogues from speaking it. The Old Testament forbids the prophecy of "smooth things." Jewish and Christian history are full of times when a word had to be spoken *against* the principalities and powers. In the face of any evil, the mandate that Albert Camus laid upon Christians is laid upon all men, whether religious or not, that they "should speak out, loud and clear, and that they should voice their condemnation in such a way that never a doubt, never the slightest doubt, could rise in the heart of the simplest man. That they should get away from abstraction and confront the blood-stained face history has taken on today."[1]

America's overwhelming share of responsibility for the "blood-stained face history has taken on today" in Vietnam, must haunt all Americans and must prompt the religious community in particular to outcry. The voice of the churches and synagogues should have been heard earlier and in clearer tones, but regardless of past omissions it must be heard now.

As we have noted, the allegiance of church and synagogue to a nation is held under a higher allegiance—allegiance to the God who is sovereign over all the nations. Often the higher allegiance can serve the lower, but sometimes they conflict. When they do, the priorities are clear: "You shall have no other gods before me" (Exodus 20:3). When the nation makes demands that go contrary to conscience or morality, the answer God expects is unequivocal: "We must obey God rather than men" (Acts 5:29). For increasing numbers of Christians and Jews, American policy in Vietnam is forcing such choices, and making it impossible to reconcile allegiance to the nation with allegiance to God.

The need to speak is thus an exercise of faith, but it is also an expression of the democratic privilege. Responsible expression of disagreement and dissent is the lifeblood of democracy, and when individuals or groups feel that their nation is pursuing a policy that is leading to world disaster, they may not retain the privilege of silence.

No purpose is served by implying that evil men have promoted America's increasing involvement in the war, or that there is a master plan designed to increase the unnecessary shedding of blood. Indeed, part of the problem is precisely the *lack* of any plan. No one planned the type of war in which we are involved. It has slowly escalated from one small move to the next small move, each presumed to be the last that would be necessary. The President and the Congress find themselves dealing with a situation all decent men abhor, but they have been reduced to the position of facing political and human problems for which they seem to be able to offer only military answers.

But the fact that no one planned it this way, that it is an accumulation of small mistakes that have grown into one

[1] *Resistance, Rebellion and Death* (New York: Knopf, 1960), p. 71.

gigantic mistake, is no reason to repeat and compound the pattern of mistakes on an ever-widening scale. That we seem nevertheless to be doing just that makes imperative the need to speak before it is too late. For it is morally indefensible to condone by silence decisions that are leading in intolerable directions.

The Increasing Anguish

Why is it that more and more Christians and Jews find it impossible to support the nation's policy of military escalation in Vietnam? There are at least four reasons for the increasing anguish.

1. The first of these is based on *the immorality of the warfare in Vietnam.* Our very right to be there is questioned, in the light of international law, by men highly placed in our government, among them Senators Morse, Church, Gore, and Gruening. But even if there were a clearcut "right," the nature of what we are doing in Vietnam must be increasingly condemned.

• This is a war in which civilian casualties are greater than military. The victims are not mainly soldiers from the other side (or from our side) but women, children, the aged, whether they are victims of bombing raids or indiscriminate jungle fire. Of the civilians killed, at least half are children. Figures on Vietnamese war dead are unreliable, but in a recent "search and destroy" operation, for example, the ratio was estimated at six civilian casualties to one Vietcong.[2] A thousand peasant homes may be destroyed in a few hours as the price for a few hundred enemy troops.[3] Returning from a recent trip to Vietnam, Professor Claude Buss reported, "I was told that U.S. activities put 30 innocent civilians into the hospital for every one wounded by the Vietcong, and that out of 100 reported casualties no more than 10 were actually Vietcong."[4] In the name of "liberation," we are destroying the very people we profess to liberate.

---

[2] *Friends Committee National Legislation Newsletter,* August–September, 1966.

[3] *New York Times,* February 16, 1966, p. 1.

[4] *Stanford Daily,* January 11, 1967.

• This is a war in which whole civilian populations are deported against their will. When our armies need space, when they think the enemy might be in a given area, they simply preempt the area, remove those who live there, destroy their homes, put them in relocation centers, level the forests, scorch the earth. In addition to the unknown numbers of dead, between 750,000 and 1,000,000 South Vietnamese civilians have been so uprooted.

• This is a war in which the use of napalm and white phosphorus has become commonplace. We now employ a superior brand of napalm which has better "adhesion" qualities. This means that the jelly from the bomb cannot be scraped off the skin, but adheres more efficiently so that the burning will produce more prolonged agony. This explosive does not distinguish between combat soldiers, nursing mothers, seven-year-old girls and eighty-year-old grandfathers.

• This is a war in which we defoliate the crops of the countryside so that the enemy cannot seek cover behind them. Since Vietnam is one of the richest and most fertile growing areas in the entire world, the policy has a certain military wisdom behind it. But the result is the despoiling of the countryside, the destruction of crop capacity for the next harvest and, because of the chemicals used, the impossibility in many areas of growing food for many years to come. If this is liberation, it is liberation for starvation and economic ruin.

• This is a war in which both sides torture prisoners to secure information, in total lack of conformity to the Geneva Convention. An accumulating mass of data makes clear that prisoners are subjected to water torture, slow drowning, starvation, being dragged behind jeeps, dropped from helicopters, and subjected to further indignities that the western mind can scarcely comprehend.

All who believe that man is made in God's image must be horrified by such crimes committed against God and man. The guilt for such deeds is not all on one side of course, but the guilt is ours far more than we dare to admit.

A war in which such actions have become commonplace, and which our leaders nevertheless defend as "honorable," is not a war that Christians and Jews can condone. We can only tremble at the thought that God is just.

2. Our moral anguish is increased by *the inconsistency between our stated aims and their actual consequences.*

• We are told that our military presence in Vietnam will stem the tide of communism. But what is it actually doing? At the very moment when "world communism" as an ideological monolith is breaking up into nationalistic societies, we are engaging in a battle against one of those societies, the intensity of which will make it increasingly necessary for other Communist societies to come to its aid. Countries that would otherwise be developing separate destinies—a fact that would be in our national self-interest—will more and more be forced to make common cause against us.

• We are told that our gradual military escalation will hasten the conclusion of the war and persuade the enemy to sue for peace. But what is it actually doing? Not only does our policy of fighting a guerrilla war with bombers (which Arthur M. Schlesinger, Jr., has compared to weeding a garden with a bulldozer) put us at a tactical disadvantage, but it also serves to increase the intensity and duration of the war, without hastening its conclusion. "By December 31, 1966, the United States had dropped a total of almost 800,000 tons of bombs on North and South Vietnam—more than Germany got during the entire Second World War." [5] The number of men, planes, bombs, air bases, and war materiel needed by us to destroy one enemy truck is almost beyond calculation. In this kind of war even the military experts suggest that five to fifteen years would be needed to "win."

• We are told that our persistent bombing of the North will cut down the infiltration of supplies to the South and break the morale of the enemy. But what is it actually doing? The sending of supplies to the South has not been effectively halted by the bombing. On February 15, 1967, Secretary of Defense McNamara told newsmen, " 'I am not prepared to

[5] *San Francisco Chronicle, This World,* February 12, 1967, p. 14.

say today' whether infiltration has declined."[6] His testimony to the Fullbright Committee has made clear that the bombing, no matter how intensive, can bring only limited results in the war.[7] The morale of the people in Hanoi is clearly not being destroyed, but solidified by the bombing, as Harrison Salisbury's reports in the *New York Times* indicate.[8]

• We are told that our widening military involvement will gain us the confidence of the rest of the world, by indicating our firmness and resolve, our unwillingness to back down in the face of aggression. But what is it actually doing? Our action in Vietnam is increasingly resented by the rest of the world. Two years ago, Walter Lippmann could report, "Today the United States is not only isolated but increasingly opposed by every major power in Asia. With the exception of Japan, which has a government, but not a people, who support our policy, all the Asian powers are against us on the issue—not only Communist China and Indonesia but the Soviet Union, India and Pakistan. [They] are quarreling to the point of war with one another but they are united in condemning our war."[9] When the United States began its bombing of the outskirts of Hanoi and Haiphong, over a year later, James Reston reported, "There is now not a single major nation in the world that supports Mr. Johnson's latest adventure in Hanoi and Haiphong."[10]

The other nations detect bankruptcy in a foreign policy which can offer only military answers to political questions. They see us rejecting diplomacy in favor of force. They see us paying lip service to the United Nations and then undermining the efforts of the United Nations to bring about a negotiated peace. They see us supporting the militaristic regime of Premier Ky in Saigon—the same Ky who said his only hero was Adolf Hitler—a regime that depends for its continuance in power, not upon the will of the people of South Vietnam, but upon the military presence of the United States. Representatives in the Peace Corps all over the world report increasing restiveness among citizens of smaller na-

---

[6] Associated Press dispatch, February 16, 1967.
[7] *San Francisco Chronicle,* February 15, 1967.
[8] December 27, 1966–January 14, 1967.
[9] *San Francisco Chronicle,* April 22, 1965.
[10] *New York Times,* July 1, 1966.

tions over our unilateral policy of deciding what is best for the Vietnamese.

3. The anguish is deepened by *the discrepancy between what we are told by our government and what we discover is actually taking place.* A "credibility gap" of increasing proportions has developed, so that it becomes harder and harder to know which statements out of Washington are true, which ones are merely offered for propaganda purposes, and which are deliberately misleading. As the National Council of Churches put it, "Conflicting policy statements by high officials have provided such confusion that there has been a continuing crisis of credibility." [11] James Reston has described the resulting bewilderment:

> The Johnson administration said it was not seeking a military solution to the war, and it is now obviously seeking precisely that. It said it was there merely to help a legitimate government defend itself, and it has ended up by replacing a military clique that is not a government, not legitimate, and is not really defending itself.
>
> Even when allowances are made for the uncertainties and moral ambiguities of warfare, the guile of this Administration, exercised in the name of high and even noble principle, is hard to match. It was not going beyond the Seventeenth Parallel in Vietnam, but went beyond. It was merely going to respond to enemy attacks on its bases, but it went over to the offensive. It was not going to get involved in a major war on the Asian land mass, but it did.
>
> The President was not even faithful to his bad resolves; he said he would not negotiate, but then offered to do so, and spoiled that by refusing to negotiate with the major elements of the enemy he faces. He has not merely misled his enemies but his friends. His old colleagues in the Congress have not forgiven him yet for tricking them into support of a blank check defense of all Southeast Asia under circumstances they could not possibly oppose. . . .
>
> A great deal [hangs] on whether the American people can trust the pronouncements of their Government, whether they can remain united on purposes they understand and

[11] *New York Times,* December 10, 1966, p. 6.

> respect, whether the allies believe Washington really wants a compromise settlement in Vietnam, or merely a surrender on its own terms . . . There is certainly little faith here in the official spoken word.[12]

Three examples of the credibility gap are worth noting.

• The most alarming discrepancy is our government's public claim that the other side gives no indication of desire to negotiate, after which we discover that such indications have been given, but that we have responded either with rebuff or with military escalation. A compilation of ten such instances has recently been published.[13] The authors presented their findings to the White House on June 22, 1966, requesting that the alarming pattern they noted (of our responding to peace feelers from the other side by military escalation) either be denied or explained. Neither denial nor explanation has been forthcoming. If peace feelers from the other side are now slow in coming, history may show that we, rather than they, are to blame. At all events, there is a disturbing discrepancy here between what we are told, and what we discover to be the actual case.

• A second discrepancy concerns the meaning of the Administration's reiterated claim that we are ready to negotiate "any time, anywhere." President Johnson made the assertion in a talk at Johns Hopkins University in April, 1965, that America was prepared to enter into "unconditional discussions" to end the war. And yet it soon became clear that the unconditional discussions had a hidden condition attached to them: they did not include a willingness to negotiate with the Vietcong, one of the main disputants in the Vietnamese struggle. Vice President Humphrey also rules out the presence of the Vietcong at peace talks by means of the vivid metaphor that one doesn't let a fox into a chicken house. So our government is actually *not* willing to engage in "unconditional discussions." The later concession that the Vietcong could be represented "in a North Vietnamese

[12] *New York Times*, July 1, 1966. © 1966 by The New York Times Company. Reprinted by permission.

[13] See Franz Schurmann, Peter D. Scott, and Reginald Zelnik, *The Politics of Escalation in Vietnam* (Boston: Beacon and Greenwich: Fawcett, 1966).

delegation"[14] is not, of course, satisfactory to the Vietcong, who feel they should be present in their own right. The issue is not simply the desirability or the undesirability of including the Vietcong in negotiations (a matter we shall later discuss) but the inaccurate impression our government has created that it has made all the concessions, and that intransigency exists only on the other side, whereas in fact it is our own intransigency that leaves the other side no choice but to state that our position is unacceptable.

• A third kind of discrepancy has widened the credibility gap. This is illustrated by the kind of information the public is given about the war. Figures of casualties, captured equipment, prisoners taken, territory conquered, planes lost, and so forth, are notoriously difficult to arrive at, and it is understandable that mistakes occasionally occur. But the high incidence of government statements later proven wrong makes trust in any government statements increasingly difficult. A critical illustration of this was the treatment of the bombing of Hanoi in December, 1966. The American public was told that Hanoi had not been bombed. It later became clear that Hanoi had been bombed. The American public was then told that although Hanoi had been bombed, only military targets had been hit and that civilian targets had been avoided. It later become clear that civilian targets as well as military targets had been hit, and that heavy losses to civilian targets and civilian population had been administered. In both cases, the corrections came not through official governmental channels, but through journalists on the scene who reported the facts the government releases had suppressed.

Such actions play into the hands of those who distrust the United States, since they can consistently discount our word as unreliable. But the continuous discovery of discrepancies between our nation's word and our nation's deed also shakes the confidence of the American people in the word of their government. This increasing deterioration of confidence in the spoken word of the nation's leaders has serious consequences, both immediate and long-range. The increasing anguish is thus a crisis of conscience concerning what we *do* know, and a crisis of confidence concerning what we do *not* know.

[14] *New York Times,* February 7, 1966.

4. Finally, the anguish is intensified not only by a recognition of what the war is doing to those we devastate, but also by a recognition of *what it is doing to us.*

• *Militarily,* our policy of escalation is leading in frightening directions. We have moved from

"technical advisers" in the South, to
token military presence in the South, to
increasing military presence in the South without bombing of the North, to
increasing military presence in the South combined with bombing of the North, to
massive military presence in the South combined with increased bombing in the North, to
massive military presence in the South combined with increased bombing in the North and shelling of the North from battleships, to
. . . to what? to military invasion of the North? to bombing the supply lines near the China border? to bombing China itself?

The direction of escalation is inexorably one-way, and there is no point at which our own national policy can logically stop short of all-out war, if that becomes necessary. The only way to go is up, and the increase of our military pressures may well make the transition to diplomatic negotiation impossible. Commenting on a new escalation begun on February 27, 1967, which consisted of mining the North Vietnamese rivers and shelling the coast from our naval ships, the *New York Times* commented editorially:

> This escalation comes when Prime Minister Wilson of Great Britain has certified that the Soviet Union is working with his Government to seek a basis for peace negotiations. It comes while Ambassador Goldberg is assuring Asia that the United States still desires "unconditional discussions" above all else. Perhaps most important, it comes when a high-level North Vietnamese delegation has arrived in Burma, where U.N. Secretary General Thant is vacationing.
>
> Perhaps none of these efforts would have produced results, but the tragedy is that the escalation will almost

certainly prevent the world from finding out whether the possibility exists for ending the fighting, the destruction and the death.[15]

• *Politically,* our policy of military escalation increasingly threatens meaningful debate about public policy. Expression of disagreement becomes equated with disloyalty. The President has on numerous occasions questioned the loyalty of those who oppose him, referring to them as "nervous Nellies." The Vice President, speaking at Stanford University in February, 1967, gave token support to the right of dissent and then asserted in almost the same breath that demonstrations of disagreement give aid and comfort to the enemy. The Secretary of State attacked the 1965 "teach-ins" of the academic community: "I sometimes wonder at the gullibility of educated men and the stubborn disregard of plain facts by men who are supposed to be helping our young to learn—especially to learn how to think." [16]

Such attitudes can only increase as the stakes get higher and the need for military victory supplants all other objectives.

• *Economically,* our policy of military escalation demands increasingly higher proportions of our nation's resources. Every dollar spent on war in Vietnam is a dollar that cannot be spent elsewhere. The simple exercise of translating the cost of the war into creative alternatives produces some sobering results:

For the cost of *one month* of the Vietnam war, we could provide four years of training for 169,000 school teachers, 125,000 nurses, and 50,000 doctors, as well as a college education for 100,000 students who could not otherwise afford it.

For the cost of *two months* of the Vietnam war, we could do the following things for international peace:

a. wipe out the $53 million deficit of the United Nations;

[15] *New York Times,* February 28, 1967, p. 34.

[16] Cited in Marvin E. Gettleman, *Vietnam* (Greenwich: Fawcett, 1965), p. 334.

b. provide 9 million tons of wheat to India to carry it through the effects of recent drought;
c. quadruple our contribution to the International Development Association;
d. double our assistance to the U.S. bilateral development loan and technical assistance program;
e. double the size of the Peace Corps;
f. almost double our contribution to the War Against Hunger planned under the 1966 Food for Peace Act.

For the cost of *four months* of the Vietnam war, we could replace 1,000,000 of the 4,000,000 substandard housing units in the United States.

For the cost of *nine months* of the Vietnam war, we could build 296,000 elementary and secondary school classrooms, and equip 656 hospital beds needed in our country.[17]

• *Morally,* our policy of military escalation is leading to an escalation of moral numbness. The more shocking things we do, the greater becomes our capacity to endure them without shock.

In World War II, for example, we learned that the Nazis had attacked civilian strongholds, killed civilians, leveled towns to the ground, deported the inhabitants, and destroyed the fields around them, in what was called a "scorched earth" policy. We were horrified to learn of such actions, and condemned people at the Nuremberg trials for their part in such crimes. And yet we have done precisely the same thing in Vietnam without any sense of national outrage. Only we didn't call it a "scorched earth" policy; we called it "Operation Cedar Falls."

What has happened to our national conscience that we can utterly condemn a policy in 1945, and wholeheartedly endorse it in 1966? What has happened to our ability to discriminate between right and wrong, when the same action is wrong if the enemy does it, but right if we do it?

How would it stand with us, if we were to be judged by the standards employed by the Charter of the International Military Tribunal at Nuremberg: "The following acts, or

[17] Figures provided by the Friends Committee on National Legislation.

any of them, are crimes coming within the jurisdiction of the Tribunal for which there shall be individual responsibility: ill-treatment of civilian population . . . murder or ill-treatment of prisoners of war . . . wanton destruction of cities, towns or villages . . . inhumane acts committed against any civilian population."

What has happened to our moral sensitivity when our own soldiers bring home dead Vietcong on the fenders of their jeeps as trophies of the hunt—and we are not disturbed?

. . . when we report the progress of the war by reference to the "body count" of Vietcong dead—and are unaware of how callously we have come to think of human life?

. . . when we read about napalm hideously disfiguring (nursing) mothers and tiny children and elderly men—and feel no shame?

. . . when we condone the torture of prisoners—and justify it on the grounds that the enemy is doing the same thing?

What will be our moral worth at the end of a war we have conducted in such a manner?

Clearing Away the Underbrush—Or, How Not to Think About Vietnam

There are, then, many reasons for increasing anguish over Vietnam that should force us to seek alternative courses of action.

But other reasons are frequently given to justify our present policy. Whatever grain of truth such reasons hold is more than offset by the false assumptions contained in them, and part of the task of the churches and synagogues must be to cut through the underbrush of misunderstanding and misinformation. Only when false assumptions have been exposed can we deal meaningfully with proposed alternatives.

At least six such assumptions are widespread:

1. *"This is a war of Communist aggression from the North, and we have a commitment to defend the South Vietnamese."*

The argument is both oversimplistic and inaccurate. As almost every study of the tangled history of the Vietnamese struggle makes clear, what has now become the war in

Vietnam did *not* begin with "Communist aggression from the North." It began as a civil war in the South.

Our main adversary in the South, the National Liberation Front, or Vietcong, is of course predominantly Communist. But some statistics about the fighting forces in the South are highly revealing. According to a bipartisan group of the Senate Foreign Relations Committee, at the end of 1965—a full year after the sharp buildup in American military effort to protect the southerners from the northern invasion—the enemy force in the South numbered about 230,000 men, of which only 14,000 were North Vietnamese, or a little over 6 per cent. Even more revealing is the statement of Senator Mike Mansfield, head of the bipartisan group: "When the sharp increase in the American military effort began in early 1965, it was estimated that only about 400 North Vietnamese soldiers were among the enemy forces in the south, which totalled 140,000 at the time." [18]

These figures and others like them make strained, at best, the attempt to justify our military presence in Vietnam as a response to Communist invasion from the North. The South Vietnamese are not primarily the victims of such aggression; they are fighting a civil war, in which they are now receiving outside aid—from North Vietnam and North America.

The matter of our "commitment" thus results from our becoming the victims of our own propaganda. As we have poured more and more troops and war materiel into South Vietnam, we have had to find new ways of justifying our presence there. We have already seen that "Communist aggression from the North" did not begin in any serious way until *after* our military presence in South Vietnam had been overwhelmingly established.

Those who try to justify our "commitment" in terms of the provisions of the 1954 SEATO treaty fail to note that there is no provision in the treaty to make our military presence mandatory—particularly to the tune of several hundred thousand men. As the Pulitzer-prize–winning historian Arthur M. Schlesinger, Jr., puts it: "No president of the United States before President Johnson interpreted the SEATO treaty as *compelling* American military intervention, and no other signatory so interprets the treaty today. In

[18] Cited in Theodore Draper, "The American Crisis," *Commentary,* January, 1967, p. 36.

short, the . . . proposition that SEATO *commits* the United States to military intervention can only be regarded as an exercise in historical and legal distortion."[19]

2. *"If we do not stop communism at this point it will spread throughout the rest of the world."*

This is sometimes described as the "domino theory"—if one nation falls to communism, the next nation will fall and then the next, with a kind of automatic inevitability. We do not hear as much about the domino theory as we used to, and even Vice President Humphrey, in a speech at Stanford University in February, 1967, said that he is not particularly impressed by it.

But this does not dispose of the *basic* presupposition behind the assertion that we must "stop communism" in Vietnam. The basic presupposition is that "communism" is a vast monolith, everywhere and always the same, and that therefore wherever one finds it, the tactic must always be to resist it by whatever means are necessary.

The presupposition overlooks one fundamental fact that the American people have great difficulty accepting: to whatever extent "world communism" was once a monolithic structure, it is so no more. The monolith is crumbling into many pieces, and the eroding force that is wearing it down is nationalism. Communism as an ideology does not keep these nations dependent upon one another; nationalism as a passionate commitment makes them desire independence. The nationalistic spirit of the Vietnamese, for example, makes them wish to be independent of China. Border disputes between China and Russia illustrate the fact that tension between the two greatest Communist powers is close to the breaking point. Yugoslavia's degree of independence from Russia is a fact our foreign policy recognizes. In other words, the fact that two nations may be "Communist" does not mean that they are aligned together, or that they have common interests that will inevitably draw them together.

It is ironic that at precisely the moment we are saying that we must "halt communism" in Vietnam, we are coming to terms with it elsewhere, working out new treaty agreements with Russia, extending trade in Eastern Europe, giving support to Tito in Yugoslavia. Elsewhere, we have clearly

[19] *The Bitter Heritage* (Boston: Houghton Mifflin, 1967), p. 12.

decided to coexist with communism, and to encourage *independent* Communist societies that will be increasingly free of the need for alliance with one another.

The irony is compounded when precisely at the time we are helping to make Communist alliances unnecessary elsewhere, our military presence in Vietnam threatens to force a new grouping of Communist alliances in that part of the world. The more we increase our military commitment in Vietnam, the more we bomb the North, the more we threaten to "flatten Hanoi," the more we speculate about a land invasion to "win" the war—the more we will force the crumbling Communist alliance to regroup and make common cause against what Communists can only interpret as the threat of "American imperialist aggression." At the time of writing, there is tremendous upheaval in Communist China; the one thing that might enable Mao Tse-Tung to recoup his losses would be his ability to reunite his country against the threat that the American military presence in Vietnam represents to China's borders.

This kind of reply, it must be added, contains an implication that makes many Americans uneasy. This is the implication that for some parts of the world a form of communism may be the political-economic structure under which people will live both now and in the future. If the United States is really willing to allow free elections in South Vietnam, for example, the chances are high that South Vietnam will go Communist. If the United States finally agrees to let the Vietcong participate in its own right in peace negotiations, it is clear that the peace settlement will contain more elements favorable to communism than if the Vietcong is not present, although without the Vietcong there is not likely to be any peace settlement at all.

Elsewhere in the world we have accepted the notion of trying to live in a peaceful, if nervous, kind of coexistence with other Communist societies. We must be prepared for this eventuality in Vietnam or face the alternative; the alternative is that we must, by sheer force of arms, impose our will on an entire nation, refuse to let the people of that nation determine their own form of government, and commit ourselves to act as a gigantic police force not only in Vietnam but everywhere else in the world where communism threatens to establish itself. If we do so, we will make it necessary for the crumbling Communist *bloc* to join forces to resist us, and the final result of such a policy will thus be to *strengthen* "world communism" at precisely the point when, apart from our intervention, it would be breaking up into nationalistic groupings.

In order to be "anti-Communist" our nation has supported dictatorships and oppressive tyrannies in various parts of the world, assuming that since communism is "godless," *any* regime opposing it is to be preferred. This mentality has made us view communism as the only real enemy of mankind today, and has blinded us to the fact that the *real* enemy is not communism but poverty. Communism is an attempt (tragically wrong, we believe) to combat poverty. The real battle we face is the battle with poverty. As long as we merely "fight communism," poverty will increase. But to the degree that we engage in a creative frontal attack on poverty, communism (which feeds on poverty) will gradually be deprived of its major appeal.

3. *"We should win the war as rapidly as possible, using whatever means are necessary to do so."*

This argument has recently been refined by Congressman L. Mendel Rivers: "We should flatten Hanoi and let world opinion go fly a kite," and by General Curtis E. Le May, who suggests that we "bomb Hanoi back into the Stone Age."

There are few notions more terrifying to the moral conscience than those based on the assumption that whoever has power is entitled to use it any way he pleases.

It is of course technically possible that by unlimited expansion of the war we could, as Ronald Reagan said in the summer of 1966, pave Vietnam over with asphalt and still have the boys home by Christmas. By pouring in manpower, planes, bombs, and tanks we could destroy everything in sight, engaging in atomic destruction that would make Hiroshima and Nagasaki look like warmup exercises. We could also keep intact our record of being the only nation ever to use the atomic bomb. Were we to do these things, we would not only destroy the country and people we claim we want to liberate, but we would almost inevitably provoke attack from other world powers, who would not condone such a naked display of brute force. Not only would Vietnam be destroyed but most of the rest of the world and mankind with it.

Such a course of action is not a true alternative save for madmen. But it is quite conceivable that public opinion may force our policymakers to step up the escalation of the war immensely, "flatten Hanoi" as Congressman Rivers suggests, and engage in increasing destruction throughout the whole of Vietnam. Even if we did so without enlarging the war into World War III, it is clear that winning such a war "as rapidly as possible" would not be a matter of a few weeks or even a few months of escalated military operations. The military experts speak in terms of years—not one or two years, but five, ten, or fifteen years—of unremitting jungle warfare before the nation would be "liberated" in the sense that no sizable portion of the enemy remained to menace it.

What would we have at the end of such a time? A decimated, destroyed land; a decimated, destroyed people; the ill will of most of the world; a national mentality so conditioned to war that rather than laying our power down we would be tempted to unleash it immediately elsewhere to avoid the repetition of similar long-range encounters. Such a "victory" would be a mockery of the word. We would have shown the world that we had more power than anyone else. We would also have shown the world that we used power more irresponsibly and cruelly than any other nation in history had ever done. World opinion would not "go fly a kite." It would rise in increasing judgment upon us. The notion of achieving "victory" at any price, is not only morally intolerable but politically and internationally self-defeating.

4. *"The policymakers have access to information not available to us. Therefore we must trust that they are doing the right thing."*

This argument represents an appropriate modesty in the face of ignorance, but its widespread acceptance would spell the end of the democratic process. The essence of the democratic process is that the leaders are accountable to the people; they must justify what they do or be voted out of office.

The fallacy of the argument is that access to information does not necessarily mean that decisions based on that information are the only decisions possible or even the correct ones.

Until recently, we assumed that the advice of the "experts" was that our present policy should be unremittingly continued. But as the Fullbright hearings of 1966 and 1967 have made clear, the "experts" are by no means of one mind about what we should be doing in Vietnam. Many Far-Eastern experts strongly disagree with our present policy. Their testimony makes clear that possession of more "facts" does not necessarily lead to the conclusion that we should escalate the war. On the contrary, those with more facts frequently suggest that we should not.

A recent example is the testimony of Professor Edwin Reischauer before the Senate Foreign Relations Committee. It has been the stated policy of our government that we are bombing the North in order to weaken the will of the North Vietnamese to resist us. But Professor Reischauer, a life-long specialist in Oriental studies and former Ambassador to Japan, points out that such action is stiffening the will of the North Vietnamese to resist us rather than diminishing it, and that the policy is thus self-defeating. An Associated Press dispatch from Washington reports: "Professor Reischauer stated that the bombing of North Vietnam was a 'psychological blunder.' 'We started it,' he said later, 'with promises that it would achieve certain results that were not achieved. It has produced a lot of political losses around the world.' "[20] Many other experts have voiced the same kind of conclusion, among them George Kennan, J. K. Galbraith, General James Gavin, Henry Steele Commager, Richard Goodwin, Professor Claude Buss, as well as a number of U.S. Senators.

Such testimony does not entitle all citizens to become self-appointed experts on Far-Eastern psychology or military strategy, but it does entitle all citizens to demand continuing debate by the experts about Far-Eastern policy, and to refuse to succumb to the prevailing opinion that the policymakers' decisions are to be uncritically accepted.

5. *"If we criticize our nation's policies, it will suggest to the rest of the world that we are divided."*

The statement is true: we *do* criticize our nation's policies,

---

[20] Associated Press dispatch, February 1, 1967.

and to that extent we *are* divided. The question is whether or not this is an unfortunate state of affairs. Those who propose the argument obviously feel that it is, and consider that such criticism is ultimately unpatriotic.

But the expression of differences of opinion is not something of which to be ashamed. It is something in which to glory. The goal of a dictatorship is that all think alike, and that differences of opinion be suppressed, by whatever means are necessary. The goal of a democracy is the free expression of differing points of view.

Those who disagree with our present policy do not do so in a carping or unpatriotic fashion. They do so because they feel that our present policy is destined to prolong rather than shorten the war. They wish to indicate that there *are* differences of opinion, so that a reassessment of our present policy can be undertaken. To insist that criticism is unpatriotic is already to have started down the path to totalitarianism, and to have forgotten that the right of public expression and the right of dissent are among the most honorable modes of democratic expression. Citizens exercise that right every time they vote a man out of public office and elect a new man in his stead. They express it every time they insist on public debate so that alternative solutions to crucial problems may be examined. Nothing would be more fatal to a democracy than to succumb to the notion that its citizens must give unquestioning support to the policymakers. For the policymakers may be wrong—politically and technically as well as morally. If they are right, then rigorous challenge, responded to by them, will strengthen their position and the nation's support of it. But if they are wrong, it is never too soon to challenge their policies.

6. *"It's a dirty, messy war, and we shouldn't have gotten into it. But now that we're there, all we can do is stay there and win."*

This is perhaps the most commonly voiced argument for our continuing presence in Vietnam. Few people "like" the war, but they are convinced that we must see it through.

The premise of the argument is self-evident: the war *is* dirty and messy and many other things beside. But the conclusion is not self-evident: that we have no choice but to continue doing dirty, messy things. It is fatalistic and wrong to argue that because we have made a series of mistakes in the past we should compound those mistakes by making more of the same kind in the future. On the contrary, if we have made a series of mistakes in the past, we should try with redoubled vigor to find ways of extricating ourselves and the Vietnamese from the ongoing consequences of those mistakes. If we believe that it was a mistake to shift our "support" in Vietnam from that of providing "technical advisers" to that of providing military troops, we are not thereby justified in accelerating our number of military troops from 50,000 to 100,000 or from a quarter of a million (250,000) to half a million (500,000).

It is hard to avoid the conclusion that our policy of military escalation is designed partly to justify earlier decisions we should not have made. And we face the difficult situation that (as Reinhold Niebuhr, Walter Lippmann, and others have pointed out) if it is hard for a policymaker to admit a mistake, it is infinitely harder for a nation to admit a mistake. To do so, it is argued, would be interpreted as a sign of national weakness, and would encourage other nations to take advantage of our indecisiveness.

And yet it can also be argued that it would be an act not of weakness but of strength, not of cowardice but of courage, for us to acknowledge that we are not omnicompetent, that we have arrived at a stalemate (for example, a war that could continue fifteen years), that we see our own limitations, and that we are willing to take some bold new initiatives that will indicate to the rest of the world the credibility of our desire to seek a negotiated peace rather than a "victory."

The proper conclusion to draw from the premise that "it is a dirty, messy war" is not "more of the same." It is rather, "We must explore every possible alternative to what we are now doing."

The Search for Alternatives

The most familiar statement of the alternatives we have in Vietnam goes as follows:

1. We can escalate rapidly, and "win the war" in the foreseeable future. But this alternative is not feasible, since it would involve immense destruction, the possibility of having

to employ nuclear warheads, and the likelihood of igniting World War III.

2. Or, we can go to the other extreme, withdraw our troops and come back home—"tuck tail and run," as President Johnson describes it. But this alternative is not feasible either, for it would involve the humiliating acknowledgment that a powerful nation had been defeated by a weak nation, it would imply that the death of American soldiers had been in vain, and it would be an open invitation to Communists to flaunt the power of the United States elsewhere as they would have done in Vietnam.

3. Therefore, since alternatives 1 and 2 are not feasible, we have no choice but to continue our present course, carefully escalating our military pressure so that the other side will realize that it cannot win and will be forced by our superior military power to accept peace on our terms.

It is far from evident that these are the only alternatives. To reject the polarities represented by alternatives 1 and 2 does not mean that one is left only with alternative 3, an alternative that is not nearly as "moderate" as it sounds, since each step of escalation makes it less and less distinguishable from alternative 1.

A more realistic statement of alternatives might be the following:

1. We can continue to fight a hard, bloody, increasingly bitter and frustrating war. If we do so, we must be prepared to do this for many years, perhaps a decade. It is a war we can conceivably "win," but at the price of destroying the land and people we presume to liberate, of scuttling the domestic programs designed to ensure minimal justice to our own dispossessed citizens, of sacrificing more and more of our young men to death (including those who are now eight-year-olds), of widening the probability that other nations will enter the conflict, of engendering increasing hostility against ourselves throughout the rest of the world, and of emerging with a "victory" incommensurate with the cost.

2. Or, we can commit ourselves unequivocally to seek *now* rather than later for a negotiated peace, realizing that history does not present us with easy choices, and that the

road to such a peace would be long and tortuous. No one should assume that a genuine declaration of intent to seek peace would magically clear up misunderstandings, that it would immediately end hostilities, that it would not demand constant scrutiny and the highest order of diplomatic *expertise.* Just as there has been frustration and heartache in our gradual escalation, so too there would be frustration and heartache in the development of new initiatives leading to a negotiated peace. Just as the risks of extending the war are great, so too the risks of seeking new initiatives for negotiated peace are great. But they might be the most important risks the American people have ever taken.

* * *

The task of the churches and synagogues at the present time is to create a climate among the rank and file across the nation that wholeheartedly accepts the second of these alternatives, and does so in such a clear and vigorous manner that the policymakers can be emboldened not merely to give it the lip service support they already do, but to refashion policy in terms of it.

Why is this the task of the synagogues and churches? The basic reason is that the synagogues and churches affirm a belief in God as the father of all men (North Vietnamese included), and affirm a belief that God has implanted his image in all men (Vietcong included). Since the Vietnamese war is a denial of both these affirmations, the churches and synagogues must be pledged to efforts to bring it to a halt.

But in addition to the fact that the churches and synagogues have an obligation to put their actions where their words are, there is a pragmatic but equally compelling reason why they must take the initiative. This is because *no one else is doing so* in the widespread fashion that is called for. Individuals are doing so—a handful of courageous Senators, numerous private citizens, some pacifist and peace groups, and increasing numbers of the academic community. But there is no ground-swell movement among the rank and file, mobilizing such opinion.

It is a tragedy that no voice of creative leadership on Vietnam is coming from the White House. Instead of statesmanship we have petulant and often angry remarks, when pleas are made to reassess our foreign policy. The Vice President is free to do little more than echo the President's position with more glowing rhetoric. The Secretary of State repeats, week by week, a position that if anything becomes increasingly intransigent.

This vacuum of creative leadership is a tragedy, and yet it is the reality of our present situation. We have no reason to expect new initiatives to come from the executive branch of our government. Nor (since their powers were effectively stripped by the Gulf of Tonkin agreement in August, 1964) is there the likelihood of effective opposition in the Senate, until the courageous few who have expressed opposition receive the kind of public mandate that will make other Senators willing to join their ranks.

This, then, is the job of the churches and synagogues—to create that mandate, to initiate a public outcry so loud and so clear that it cannot be ignored.

The voice must speak in terms that will be heard. It is one thing to express moral indignation, to get oneself "on record" as opposing the brutality of war. That may purge the individual conscience, but if it represents only 5 per cent of the voting public it will not be taken very seriously in Washington. What the churches and synagogues must do is to articulate a position that can command the support of 51 per cent of the voters, for such a voice will be taken *very* seriously in Washington. It need not mean, and should not mean, a program worked out in infinite detail—for churchmen have no necessary *expertise* in such matters. But it must mean at least a series of "next steps" on which there can be sufficient agreement that (leaving the details with the policymakers, where they belong) the policymakers can be assured that they have a mandate to take new initiatives to lead toward a negotiated peace, and that the American people not only request but demand that such initiatives be taken.

Tactically, this means no lessening of moral indignation and concern, but it means also a mode of speech that is not so emotional or judgmental that it serves only to alienate those whom it should attract;

it means seeking a broad base of support, and making common cause not only with those who inhabit the churches and synagogues, but with all who seek a way out of our present impasse;

it means adopting positions that may seem less "prophetic" than the purists would espouse, but that are adopted out of concern to be politically effective and not merely prophetically pure.

What, then, could we say and do as a nation that would convince the rest of the world that we do "commit ourselves unequivocally to seek now rather than later for a negotiated peace"?

How Can We Make Our Intent Credible to Others?

Most Americans would agree that a negotiated peace is desirable, and that the sooner the better. But we face the grave problem that the rest of the world is skeptical of our sincerity in this matter. Our claim that we really want peace is no longer credible. The reasons for this are clear to the rest of the world, if not to us: We have been engaging in an increasingly violent war, we have hedged our proposals for negotiations with conditions unacceptable to the other side, we have responded to peace feelers from the other side with military escalation, and when we have briefly tried to give a sign of good intentions (such as stopping the bombing of the North), this new posture has not been retained for long enough to convince the other side, or the rest of the world, that we really mean it.

Many Americans feel that we have done all that can be expected of us to bring about negotiations, and that the next move is up to the other side. But such an attitude can only prolong the war. We, as the stronger nation, must give more conclusive evidence than we yet have that we desire peace above all things and that we are willing to expend infinite energy in the search for ways to bring it about.

What we must establish as our sincere intent is something like the following: *the assurance that we genuinely wish to negotiate, that we seek a peace without victory, and that we are not therefore trying to win at the conference table what we have been unable to win on the battlefield.*

How are we to give credibility to this intent? There are a number of suggestions, endorsed by world statesmen, U Thant, congressmen, diplomats, and various religious groups, that deserve the support of churches and synagogues. They have the advantage of being specific and immediate, and yet of laying a groundwork that could have immense long-range benefits as well. A growing consensus of support for them would make it impossible for the policymakers to ignore them any longer, and would force our nation to re-evaluate its present catastrophic policy and move in new directions. Four of these will be described:

1. It is increasingly clear that one indispensible prerequisite to the gaining of credibility is the willingness of the United States *unconditionally to cease the bombing of North Vietnam.*

Why is this so important? It is important because we are presently at an impasse. We have said that we will not cease the bombing until there is some sign from the other side of willingness to negotiate. The other side has said it will give no further sign of willingness to negotiate until we cease the bombing.

The impasse will persist until it is overcome by a fresh initiative. The United States, as the stronger nation, has the obligation and the opportunity to take that initiative. Otherwise, the impasse remains and the war escalates. The rest of the world has little reason to trust our intent, apart from such an initiative. We have stopped bombing briefly in the past, for four days, five days, and once for thirty-seven days. But even the impact of a thirty-seven–day lull was incommensurate with the impact of the months of steady bombing that had preceded it.

Should we seize the initiative and stop again, we have no right to expect an immediate response from the other side. We will have to be prepared to wait a long time, hoping that the credibility of our intent can be established this time by the fact that we do wait. During the interval, of course, we will have to use all the diplomatic resources at our disposal to explore and re-explore every hint and clue that may appear. We can also believe that world opinion will steadily build up to urge a positive response from the other side.

No one should be romantic about such a step. It entails risks, and no proponents should pretend that it does not. The risks are (a) that even if we stop the bombing no response will be forthcoming, and (b) that during the interval the other side will simply build up its supply lines for more furious battle in the future. But since no response has been forthcoming during the bombing, that situation cannot deteriorate further, and there is always the possibility that it will improve. At least, the cessation of the bombing creates a climate more conducive to the possibility of peace talks, and that is a risk eminently worth taking. As far as the building up of supplies is concerned, no one presumes that the United States will be idle during such a period. The proportions of power will not materially change; what will be different is that fewer people will be dying.

The suggestion is not far-out, "Communist-inspired," or evidence of lack of patriotism. Those who still feel that it is must take account of the fact that it was recently articulated in that eminently respectable journal, *The Saturday Evening Post:*

> [It is not enough] for the leader of the world's most powerful nation to wring his hands in a show of helplessness and say that he has no alternatives. The alternative to war is peace; the alternative to bombing civilian villages is to stop bombing civilian villages; the alternative to complaining that one has no choice is to investigate what the choices are . . . .
>
> [As a result of the survey of World War II strategic bombing] two conclusions seem obvious: First, that strategic bombing, far from breaking a people's spirit, tends to make them rally around their leaders; second, that strategic bombing is one of the clumsiest, messiest, bloodiest and least efficient ways of waging war . . . .
>
> On all grounds, our policy of bombing North Vietnam seems the least effective and least defensible aspect of our war in Vietnam. Whatever commitment we may have to defend the south can scarcely be interpreted as a commitment to attack the north; whatever commitment President Johnson inherited from his predecessors was no commitment like this . . . .
>
> We ourselves have asked Secretary-General U Thant of the United Nations to take whatever steps he can to bring about a negotiated settlement, and U Thant almost immediately declared that the first step would be for the U.S. to stop bombing North Vietnam, not for a brief "pause" but permanently and unconditionally. Surely,

the Administration would be well advised to consider his proposal with the utmost seriousness.[21]

But the administration has not considered the proposal "with utmost seriousness." It has consistently closed its mind to such a suggestion, and adopted a policy of military escalation in its stead, with the result that after two years of mammoth escalation the war has become mammoth and peace is further away than ever.

2. A second initiative on our part could help create a climate conducive to negotiations. It is an outgrowth of the first and can therefore be discussed more briefly. This would be a decision on our part to *deescalate the war elsewhere.*

Why is this so important? Because the real "enemy" is in the South, not the North, and some demonstration of our intent is needed where the conflict is most severe. Various kinds of deescalation could be worked out in ways that would not endanger military and civilian personnel. One of the most widely discussed of these has been the suggestion that we withdraw to a certain geographical perimeter, making clear that, while we will defend the lives of those within it, we will not engage in offensive warfare beyond it. Such a move, or a more expertly conceived variant of it, could be offered to the world as an indication of our genuine desire for peace rather than military victory.

3. If the above initiatives could help gain credibility for our intent to seek a negotiated peace, a third initiative could help to reassure those who feel that we will simply use the conference table to gain a victory diplomatically that we could not gain militarily. This would be our unambiguous declaration of willingness to *accept the Vietcong at the negotiation table as a partner in its own right.*

Why is this so important? It is important because without it, our offer of "unconditional discussions" simply does not ring true. To say we will negotiate only with *some* of the combatants in the war is to be laying down conditions in advance of negotiation that cannot possibly be acceptable

[21] "Vietnam: A First Step," editorial, *The Saturday Evening Post,* February 11, 1967, p. 86. Excerpted and reprinted by special permission of *The Saturday Evening Post.* © 1967, The Curtis Publishing Company.

to the other combatants. It leaves us in the position of appearing to say, "We are willing to negotiate. Why aren't you?" when in reality it says, "We will negotiate only on terms overwhelmingly favorable to us." It thus suggests to the rest of the world that we are not serious about a desire to negotiate, and that we would rather run the risks of an escalating war than the risks of negotiation.

There are those who will reply that letting the Vietcong into the conference room is a risk we should not take, as foolish as letting a fox into a chicken coop, to repeat Mr. Humphrey's phrase. But we should remember that the precondition for negotiation is not that all partners agree; if they did, there would be no need to negotiate. The precondition for negotiation is a willingness to hear all sides of a dispute; and that we cannot possibly do if the Vietcong is not present in its own right.

4. Another way we could establish the credibility of our intent would be to make unambiguously clear that we are willing to *employ the resources of any and all international organizations* in the search for peace. This would include, for example, an increasing role for the United Nations, and such things as a recognition of the potential role of the International Control Commission in reducing ground hostility by providing an international presence under cover of which foreign troops might ultimately be withdrawn from Vietnam.

Why is this so important? It is important because although we have given lip service to a possible role for the United Nations, we have continually thwarted its efforts to establish negotiations. The following account illustrates the plight in which U Thant finds himself caught:

> Thant made three direct appeals to the Johnson Administration on Vietnam, all of which were rebuffed in a way that suggests that the Administration's much-advertised search for negotiations is fraudulent.
>
> In capsule form, the story is as follows: After the death of Diem, Thant urged a broadly-based and representative government in the South, and passed on the names of exiles who could help in forming one. Washington thanked him and did nothing about it. In August of 1964, Thant called on Dean Rusk, and came away with the feeling that the U.S. was receptive to the idea of private con-

versations between Hanoi and Washington. Thant therefore proposed it to Hanoi and got agreement from Ho Chi Minh. Adlai Stevenson passed the word on to Washington, but no word came back. Thant was not alarmed: the Goldwater–Johnson campaign was in full swing. Surely a favorable reply would come after the election. But by January 8—nearly five months after Ho had agreed to talks—there was still no word from Washington. Stevenson and Thant took some steps on their own. The Ambassador asked the Secretary General to suggest a place for the talks. Burma, one of four countries where Washington and Hanoi are both represented, agreed to play host. Everything was now set. Stevenson passed the word to Washington and the answer came back—No. Washington was afraid that the regime in South Vietnam would be demoralized by even a rumor of talks. Moreover, Washington replied that it had checked through the Canadian representative in the International Control Commission in Hanoi and had been told that Ho was not interested in talks. Later, the Canadians let it be known privately that they had made no such check.

Early in April, following Russian efforts to set up talks, seventeen non-aligned nations appealed for negotiations. President Johnson replied that the U.S. stood ever ready for "unconditional discussions." Thant noted press reports that North Vietnam was still ready for discussions, under certain stated conditions. He drafted an appeal for a cease-fire and passed it on privately to Washington with the statement that he would be willing to consider any alterations or modifications the U.S. might wish. He never got a reply of any kind . . . .[22]

During the bombing lull over Tet (the Buddhist New Year) in early February, 1967, other attempts at negotiations were being carried on. But in the midst of them the Secretary of State held a press conference making clear that the United States would proceed on a unilateral course. Donald Grant describes the impact of this decision at the U.N.:

Secretary of State Dean Rusk has succeeded in discouraging all hopes that there can be any negotiations

[22] "U Thant's Secret," editorial, *The Commonweal,* December 16, 1966, pp. 311-12.

soon looking toward the end of the war in Vietnam. This was the reaction of United Nations diplomats to Rusk's press conference late yesterday. It is assumed that this effect was intended.

Another effect, whether intended or not, is to discourage efforts toward peace involving UN diplomats, including those of Arthur J. Goldberg, chief United States delegate at the UN, diplomats thought. Goldberg, it is reported, was as shocked by the tone and content of Rusk's press conference as were other diplomats here.

Rusk, certainly for the moment, closed any possible doors to further peace efforts by UN Secretary General U Thant, it can be reported. The Secretary General would, of course, take any action he could to get peace talks started, but he sees no opening now.[23]

It is clear even from these brief examples that it is not enough for our government merely to repeat that it has always sought the help of the United Nations in the past. Our past actions give no reason for anyone to take such a declaration seriously. There will need to be a new openness, a new humility on our part, when the possibilities of United Nations help loom on the horizon, and the American people must make clear to the policymakers that they are willing to place considerably more faith in the U.N. than Washington has done in the past. Vietnam is not just an American problem to be solved by Americans alone. It is an international problem which America has immensely complicated. We cannot therefore seek to solve it in the same unilateral way that we have aggravated it; at whatever point any help from outside our country appears, we must cooperate to the utmost.

* * *

These are four types of action, then, by means of which the United States might be able to regain credibility for its announced aim to seek a negotiated peace. Some will think the proposals too tame and pedestrian, and hardly the "bold initiatives" that are called for. But it should be remembered that they are bold indeed compared to what the United

[23] *St. Louis Post-Dispatch*, February 10, 1967, p. 1C.

States has done so far, and they represent no more than a series of next steps to break the present impasse.

Even by the time this appears in print, other specific proposals may have emerged that call for public support. But any proposals should be judged by the degree to which they meet the following criteria:

a. some act or acts of initiative on the part of the United States, taken at risk, to make absolutely clear our willingness to shift from exclusively military action to diplomatic action;
b. clear assurance that we do not intend to use the conference table to try to win a victory for ourselves; and
c. firmer reason for the world to believe that we will treat with utmost seriousness any attempt by agencies other than ourselves to bring about the beginning of negotiations.

Even the achievement of these goals would not end the crisis in Vietnam; it would simply put that crisis in a different focus. It would not mean that the problems had been solved, but it would mean that the disputants had agreed that the problems were solvable. It would not mean that the boys would immediately come home, or that the domestic budget could immediately be fleshed up, or that money needed for the war in Vietnam would immediately be diverted elsewhere. But it would mean that the Vietnamese situation was beginning to be dealt with by diplomacy rather than destruction. The road would be hard, the setbacks many, the disappointments great. But creative and constructive ends would be in view, and a situation of despair would begin to be transformed into a situation of hope. For the risks of war would gradually be replaced by the risks of peace.

For these reasons, then, a strong obligation rests on the churches and synagogues to create a base of public support for such proposals, so that our policymakers will take the steps they are as yet unwilling to take.

We must therefore turn to some of the ways in which such support could be mobilized, and some of the further ways in which the churches and synagogues could speak and act creatively in the midst of a situation that has become so terribly destructive.

Specific Tasks for Churches and Synagogues

There are a number of ways in which churches and synagogues can relate more directly to the decision-making processes that are crucial or a resolution of the conflict in Vietnam.

1. *The issue must be forced on the conscience of the churches and synagogues, so that together they can force it on the conscience of the nation.*

Care must be taken not to let this initial activity become the only activity; we could spend so much time reminding the churches and synagogues of their duty that history would pass us all by. But those within the religious communities must keep pressing their denominational leaders, their diocesan officials, their synagogue officers, their pastors, priests and rabbis, to put the issue of Vietnam high on the agenda of priorities for sermons, meetings, discussions, community mobilizations, and so forth. The concern of the religious community has been focused in part by the kinds of statements included in the Appendix to this volume. But stronger and more specific statements are needed, so that those within the religious community can be encouraged to put their actions where their words are, knowing that their churches and synagogues are behind them. No national religious body should be able to conclude its annual meeting this year or next without considering Vietnam and pressing new imperatives on the consciences of its members.

The most important thing about such action is that it be done *ecumenically*. As the very format of this book suggests, Vietnam is a problem for Catholics, Protestants, and Jews together, not separately. The things that separate us elsewhere do not separate us here. While Christians and Jews disagree about the significance of a first-century Jew, they do not disagree about the significance of a twentieth-century Vietnamese. While Catholics and Protestants disagree about the authority of the voice emanating from the See of Peter, they do not disagree about the importance of heeding that voice when it pleads with our President to end the devastation of which our nation is guilty.

Catholics, Protestants, and Jews represent different theological traditions, but they all embody the shared tradition of a common humanity, united in anguish and increasingly in outrage, and from that tradition they can already speak as one. It is imperative that they do so. When local councils of churches lay Vietnam on the conscience of their communities, they should be careful to enunciate a position that pastors, priests, and rabbis can affirm together. When meetings are held on Vietnam, care should be taken to include participation by representatives of all faiths. In every way possible, the religious communities must make clear that they share a common voice and make a common witness.

The churches and synagogues can also do more to sensitize the consciences of their individual members. Due to the initiative of a group of St. Louis clergy and laymen, for example, a nationwide "fast for the rebirth of compassion" was held during the first three days of Lent, 1967. The fast did not change our foreign policy, but it served notice that at least a million Christians and Jews were concerned enough to make this kind of token identification with the poor and hungry of Vietnam. Those who participated found that the experience of being hungry made them all the more concerned to press for changes in our foreign policy that could end hunger and devastation in Southeast Asia.

The churches and synagogues can also promise and ensure support to individuals who feel compelled to register more emphatic protest as individuals than is likely to come from groups. Many individuals, for example, the present writer included, are coming to feel that nothing short of the threat of defeat in 1968 will persuade the present Administration to change its policy. Christians and Jews may agree on this but disagree on the strategy it entails. Some will press for a "palace revolution" within the Democratic Party that will unseat Johnson and Humphrey at the convention. Others will push the Republican Party to nominate a candidate pledged to work for negotiations. Still others will want to organize a protest vote in favor of an independent candidate who could not win, but whose high number of votes would serve notice to both parties that the group of Americans urging negotiation is too large to be discounted. Those who are wrestling with such choices deserve support from the religious community, even though it is unlikely that the religious community will overwhelmingly endorse a single option among the three.

2. *The churches and synagogues must mobilize enough support for specific next steps so that our policymakers will be forced to move in new directions.*

It is not enough for the churches and synagogues to come out in favor of peace. Everybody is in favor of peace. What is necessary is that an increasingly articulate body of widely shared opinion be communicated to Washington, indicating not only dissatisfaction with our present policy, but urging specific next steps that can command wide support among the rank and file. The four suggestions of the previous section for the regaining of credibility offer a series of specifics that already command wide support across the world but will not be favorably received in Washington until the policymakers are convinced that the proposals have the support of a broad spectrum of public opinion here at home.

The way of registering this kind of opinion is old and unspectacular, but it is effective. It consists of inundating the policymakers with expressions of opinion, individual letters, group letters, telegrams, statements of deliberative bodies, accounts of local meetings from the press forwarded to Washington to indicate what the people back home are thinking, and so on. Three kinds of pressure seem crucial in relation to Vietnam:

- Increasing protest against our present policy must continually be registered with those who administer that policy —President Johnson, Vice President Humphrey, Secretary of State Rusk, and others.

- Pressures must be exerted on those, particularly in Congress, who have not committed themselves irrevocably to our present policy of military escalation. Senator Fullbright has estimated that there are between thirty and forty Senators who could still go one way or the other on Vietnam. If a congressman's position is not already known, the chances are that he is in this category, and nothing is more likely to help him make up his mind than vigorous mail from home.

• Frequently neglected, and yet fully as important as the other two, is the continued expression of support for those in public life who have already committed themselves to seek for alternatives to our present policy. These men have taken positions that isolate them from the main body of opinion in Washington, and they deserve continued reassurance that an increasing number of people support them. This group includes Senators Fullbright, Morse, Church, Gruening, Hartke, McCarthy, Young, Hatfield, Clark, McGovern, Gore, Nelson, Javits, Robert Kennedy, and others.

The question of our policy in Vietnam will not finally be settled in the local church hall or in the local pulpit or at the local rally. It will finally be settled in Washington but it will only be settled in Washington as the voices of local protest from local hall, pulpit, or rally are finally registered there.

3. In addition to such political involvement, there are *nonpolitical activities through which churches and synagogues can engage in reconciliation and rebuilding even in the midst of destructiveness.*

• Americans bear a special burden of responsibility for *war-burned and war-injured Vietnamese children.* It is our napalm and white phosphorus bombs that have wrought such hideous damage to the innocents in this war. A group of doctors, with the support of many people in public life, has organized The Committee of Responsibility, to begin to make amends for the evil we have done, by seeking facilities for the treatment of these victims, transporting them to the United States or other countries for the extensive medical care that is unavailable in Vietnam. The Committee needs public support, beds in local hospitals, participating doctors (particularly plastic surgeons), foster homes, and money. There are few things closer to elemental human compassion and mercy than the proposals of the Committee of Responsibility. No church or synagogue should be able to escape direct involvement in raising funds and offering resources to it. (Further information is available from The Committee of Responsibility, 777 United Nations Plaza, Room 7F, New York, N.Y. 10017.)

• Churches and synagogues have an ongoing responsibility to witness to the existence of reconciling love across the boundaries of conflict even while the war is going on. An opportunity for doing this is provided through *Meals of Reconciliation.* At such meals, tea and rice alone are served, to symbolize an identification with Asians, and each person contributes at least the cost of the meal he would ordinarily have eaten. The money, administered through the International Red Cross, the Fellowship of Reconciliation, or similar agencies, is used to ship medical supplies to the victims of warfare in *both* North and South Vietnam. Such action, therefore, registers concern not only for those on "our side" who have been injured, but also for those whom "our side" has injured.

• The treatment of *prisoners of war* must be another ongoing concern of churches and synagogues. The inhumane treatment of prisoners, in both North and South, has been one of the most brutalizing aspects of the war, and all honest accounts of it are full of descriptions of the debasing and bestial practices engaged in by both sides. The collective pressure of the leaders of the American religious communities upon international religious agencies can help to create more effective programs for the speedy repatriation and humane treatment of prisoners, special attention to their nutritional and medical needs, and, to the degree that systems of inspection are permitted, an elimination of the inhumane methods often used to extract information and express vindictiveness.

4. *Certain ongoing areas of principle remain the particular responsibility of the churches and synagogues.*

• One of these is a concern for *constraint.* It is not only the treatment of prisoners that illustrates the problem, for constraint tends to disappear everywhere the longer modern war is waged. Human life becomes cheaper and cheaper as the stakes in victory get higher and higher, and even the most finely drawn lines, beyond which human debasement should never go, tend to be lost in the pressures of warfare. Certain principles of international law, as embodied in the agreements of Geneva and the Hague, the Nuremberg judgments, the charter of the United Nations, and other such documents, are increasingly violated by both sides in Vietnam. These include such things as the destruction of civilian life and property, the use of gas and other chemicals, and the treatment of prisoners of war.

The principle of constraint cannot be abandoned by our nation without its becoming so brutalized that there will be little worth salvaging from a war won in such dehumanizing fashion. An example of the concern that can be registered here is the recently circulated "Open Letters to the Catholic Clergy and Laity of the United States." In addition to other matters, it specifically states:

> We ask you to join us in condemning emphatically and unambiguously at least the following aspects of American intervention in Vietnam:
> 1. Indiscriminate bombing which grossly destroys any sufficient distinction between combatant and civilian;
> 2. The use of napalm and fragmentation bombs;
> 3. Defoliation tactics and crop destruction, which leave the countryside a ravaged wasteland;
> 4. The torture of prisoners in any form whatsoever.

• The churches and synagogues have an ongoing responsibility to protect the rights of the *conscientious objector*. While conscientious objection to war has been a minority witness in organized Christianity and Judaism, it is central to the full heritage of both faiths. Those who preach the love of neighbor have a particular obligation to defend those who take them at their word and demand the right to exemplify love of neighbor by refusing to kill.

There is a particularly high incidence of conscientious objection in relation to the Vietnam war, much of it disguised by the fact that conscientious objectors are often given deferment on other grounds. But there are increasing numbers of young men who align themselves with the statement of over one hundred student body presidents sent to President Johnson in December, 1966: "Unless this conflict can be eased, the United States will find some of her most loyal and courageous young people choosing to go to jail rather than to bear the country's arms . . . ."[24]

[24] *New York Times*, December 30, 1966, p. 4.

When an individual takes a stand against war on the basis of conscience, the religious community has an absolute obligation to support him in that stand. This means not only providing religious counsel, but also making legal counsel available to him, particularly when he does not fall within the conventionally circumscribed boundaries of past conscientious objection. The supremacy of conscience is a precious dimension of what makes people both human and humane, and no pressures from government must ever be allowed to force the churches and synagogues to cease their support of those who oppose the war.

• Whatever direction the war takes, there will be *military appropriations bills* before Congress each year. In the past, such bills have been an all-or-nothing package: either the congressman voted for the whole amount or he voted for nothing at all. Congressmen, and their constituencies through them, should be allowed more discriminating choices than this. A military appropriations bill should be the occasion for fresh debate on national policy, with an opportunity to vote for various levels of support, so that some control over national policy can be exercised at this point. Three such levels could easily be distinguished: (a) an appropriation to maintain the current level of military operations, (b) an appropriation to finance new stages of military buildup and (if the Vietnam war is still continuing) proposed degrees of escalation, and (c) an appropriation to provide only the type of military and civilian security that would be needed during a period of prolonged negotiations.

5. *Preparation for the rebuilding of war-torn Vietnam, once negotiations are under way, must be an ongoing concern of churches and synagogues.*

We who have destroyed so much will have a particular responsibility to help rebuild what we have destroyed. Those with special skills in such fields as education, land reform, housing, nutrition, medicine, and job training can be preparing now to help in Vietnam during the long and involved period of negotiations. The resources of Catholic, Protestant, and Jewish relief agencies will need to be coordinated for such ventures, and foundations should be urged to support ecumenically sponsored projects of reconstruction.

It is important to realize, however, that such acts on our

part will have enduring meaning *only* when the United States has pledged itself to seek a negotiated peace in terms more courageous than it has yet exhibited. The full worth of acts of reconciliation can only come after negotiations are under way. Otherwise our small gestures of concern can only be interpreted as condoning our massive acts of ongoing destruction.

Other creative possibilities can be developed for both the public and private sectors of our nation. In addition to massive federal funds, there will be opportunities for individuals with special skills to give such help as the Vietnamese wish to accept. Members of Congress and the legal professions, for example, could offer their services, under the auspices of Asian members of such bodies as the International Parliamentary Union, for whatever counsel the Vietnamese desire in the development of the constituent assembly, and many other projects can be developed in which members of the religious community can work alongside other citizens.

In all such ventures, however, there is a danger to which Americans must be particularly sensitive. This is the temptation of using acts of mercy as a means of exporting the American Way of Life, and of imposing an alien culture, whether American or merely western, on the Vietnamese. It is crucial therefore that the leadership in such activities be out of our hands, and we must ask that our help be channeled through international agencies, indicating our willingness to serve only as others choose to use us, and not as we dictate.

We must convey by word, and even more by deed, our desire to let the Vietnamese be the arbiters of their own destiny, and insist only on such temporary international controls as will be needed to insure that injustices are prevented or are properly rectified. We who have dictated the terms of our military occupation so arbitrarily must make every effort to insure that our peacetime presence is at the will and pleasure of the people to whom we owe so much and who have such an understandable right to be suspicious of every gift we offer.

Our Ongoing Responsibility

We have an obligation, Christians and Jews alike, to get on record and insist that our fellow citizens do likewise. Silence and inaction are no longer merely irresponsible. They are immoral.

But the obligation is to do more than simply getting on record. The obligation is to influence policy, to register an outcry that cannot be ignored, to create the climate of opinion in which mistakes can be acknowledged and new directions sought. We must continually reaffirm our responsibility to urge that new direction. We must continue to lay this burning concern upon the consciences of our religious bodies, through our local congregations, our denominational agencies, our councils of churches, and our involvement in civic groups, so that increasing pressure can be brought to bear, through the pulpit, the public forum, the mass media, and the ballot box, upon those in public life who make our policy decisions.

We of the churches and synagogues, who should for years have been sensitizing the conscience of the nation, bear a particularly heavy burden of guilt for what has happened so far, and therefore bear a particularly heavy burden of responsibility for righting that wrong, and initiating a new direction.

The word that is spoken to us, and must be spoken to our nation through us, is an old word. It is a biblical word, one that dominates both the Jewish and the Christian Scriptures. It is the word "Repent!" Before we dismiss it as old-fashioned, we should be reminded of what it means. It means "Turn about, begin again, make a fresh start." That is what we are called upon to do. It is not easy for the individual, it is harder for the church or synagogue, it is hardest of all for the nation. But there is no hope, literally no hope, save on the other side of that.

As we face a difficult and dangerous period in the history of man we must remember that our task is not to assign blame for the past, but to accept responsibility for the future; not to cast the stone of condemnation, but to offer the helping hand of reconciliation; not to proceed self-righteously and vindictively, but to walk humbly and repentantly.

We who are so deeply involved in the immensity of the present war must have the courage to initiate new steps that will lead to peace. If we do not take those steps, we can be sure that God will judge us harshly and that he will hold us accountable for the horror we continue to unleash.

But if we do turn about, if we do seek to undo whatever measure we can of the wrong that has been done, then we can also be sure that as we begin to walk that long and hard and often discouraging road, God himself will be with us, to guide and chasten and sustain us, and that he will deign to use even us in restoring some portion of the divine creation we have so grievously misused.

Appendix

Statement of the Synagogue Council of America
January, 1966

Along with Americans of all faiths, we confront with deep sorrow the loss of American and Vietnamese lives, both North and South, and the suffering of the civilian population in that agonized and war-torn country. Our religious conscience compels us to exert every influence so that the action in Viet Nam can be moved from the battlefield to the negotiating table.

We therefore note with gratification that President Johnson has on numerous occasions committed the Administration to the principle of unconditional discussions leading to the negotiation of the cessation of hostilities and a peace settlement.

. . . The danger of new pressures for unlimited escalation of the war resulting from impatience and disappointment is grave indeed. Such an escalation would not only fail to achieve our goals, but would ultimately involve the world in a war of mutual destruction.

We therefore urge the Administration:

—to persist in its present efforts to pursue every possible avenue, including channels of the United Nations, that may create more favorable circumstances in which negotiations can begin;

—to steadfastly adhere to the principle that there cannot be a satisfactory military solution to this problem, and until a negotiated settlement is achieved, not to permit a change in the restrained character of this conflict through military escalation.

We further recommend that the United States should consider the following suggestions:

1. Request the United Nations to begin negotiations wherever and whenever possible for a cease-fire agreement (including cessation of terrorist activities) under United

Nations supervision, among the governments of the United States, of North and South Viet Nam, including representation for the National Liberation Front, and other interested parties, and to convene a peace conference to explore the basis of a settlement of the long-term issues and the means to give such a settlement effective international guarantees.

2. Make clear that a primary objective of a settlement of the Viet Nam conflict is the independence of South Viet Nam from outside interference, with complete liberty to determine the character of its future government by the result of a peaceful, free and verified choice of its people.

3. Declare itself in favor of the phased withdrawal of all its troops and bases from the Vietnamese territory, if and when they can be replaced by adequate international peacekeeping forces, composed of military contingents capable of maintaining order while the peace settlement is being carried out.

4. Make available, through Congress, in fulfillment of the President's proposal, immediate reconstruction assistance and long-range economic development funds for Southeast Asia, preferably through an effective international organization in which the beneficiary governments fully participate.

We do not lay claim to moral certitude and refrain from moral dogmatism in this complex and agonizing situation. Within the range of religious commitment and concern, differences as to specific policies can and do exist. We recognize that those who see the need for checking Communist subversion by military means are no less dedicated to the cause of a just world peace than those who believe the United States must cease hostilities in Viet Nam. We do believe, however, that the imperatives of our religious commitments call for the recommendations we prayerfully put forward and commend to the attention of our synagogues throughout the land.

Rabbi Seymour J. Cohen, *President*
SYNAGOGUE COUNCIL OF AMERICA

Statement of the Central Committee of the World Council of Churches, meeting in Geneva, February 8-17, 1966

In order to keep human sufferings to a minimum and to contribute to negotiations, we set forth the following measures which we believe should be undertaken as promptly as possible:

(1)

That the United States and South Vietnam stop bombing of the North and North Vietnam stop military infiltration of the South.

(2)

That the United States of America now announce its commitment to a withdrawal of its troops, phased in accordance with provisions of a peace-keeping machinery under international auspices and deemed adequate in the judgment of the international authority.

(3)

That all parties recognize the necessity of according a place in the negotiations both to the Government of South Vietnam and to the National Liberation Front (Vietcong) in proportions to be determined, and that arrangements be encouraged for negotiation between the Government of South Vietnam and the National Liberation Front in the hope that there may be found a negotiating authority representative of all South Vietnam.

(4)

That North and South Vietnam develop greater flexibility in the initiation of and response to negotiation proposals.

(5)

That all parties give every possible protection to noncombatants and relieve the plight of those suffering from the fighting.

(6)

That all parties recognize the extent to which what is happening in Vietnam is part of a social revolution and that, freed from foreign intervention, Vietnam, both North and South, ought to be in a position to determine its own future, with due consideration of the demands of peace and security in Southeast Asia.

(7)

That all parties recognize the futility of military action for the solution of the underlying political, social and economic problems of Vietnam and the necessity of massive and generous development programs.

(8)

That in order to relieve present international tension the United States review and modify its policy of "containment" of Communism, and Communist countries supporting "wars of liberation" review and modify their policy.

(9)

That every effort be made to bring the 570 million people of China, through the Government in power, the People's Republic of China, into the world community of nations in order that they may assume their reasonable responsibility and avail themselves of legitimate opportunity—to provide an essential ingredient for peace and security not only in Southeast Asia, but throughout the entire world.

(10)

That another cease-fire be mutually and promptly agreed upon of sufficient duration to serve as a cooling-off period and as an opportunity for testing possibilities of negotiation—with a considerably enlarged unit of the International Control Commission (India, Canada and Poland) and to insure that cease-fire commitments are honored.

Excerpts from the Encyclical Christi Matri *of Pope Paul VI*
September 15, 1966

. . . The danger of a more serious and extensive calamity hangs over the human family and has increased, especially in parts of eastern Asia where a bloody and hard-fought war is raging. So We feel most urgently that We must once again do what We can to safeguard peace. We are also disturbed by what We know to be going on in other areas, such as the growing nuclear armaments race, the senseless nationalism, the racism, the obsession for revolution, the separations imposed upon citizens, the nefarious plots, the slaughter of innocent people. All of these can furnish material for the greatest calamity. . . .

As you well remember, last year We flew to North America to speak about the most desirable blessing of peace at the General Assembly of the United Nations, before a very distinguished audience representing almost every nation [Cf. TPS XI, 47-57—*Ed.*]. We warned against allowing some to be inferior to others, and against allowing some to attack others. Instead, all should devote their efforts and zeal to the establishment of peace. Even afterwards, moved by apostolic concern, We did not stop urging those upon whom this great matter depends to ward off from mankind the frightful disaster that might result.

Now once again We raise Our voice "with a loud cry and with tears," [Heb 5,7.] urgently beseeching those who rule over nations to do everything they can to see to it that the conflagration spreads no farther but rather is completely extinguished. We do not doubt that all men who want what is right and honorable—whatever their race, color, religion and social class—feel the same as We do.

Therefore, let all those responsible bring about the necessary conditions for the laying down of arms before the possibility of doing so is taken away by the pressure of events. Those in whose hands rests the safety of the human race should realize that in this day and age they have a very grave obligation in conscience. Mindful of their own nation, of the world, of God and history, let them examine their own consciences. Let them realize that in the future their names will be blessed if they wisely succeed in complying with this exhortation.

In the name of the Lord We cry out to them to stop. Men must come together and get down to sincere negotiations. Things must be settled now, even at the cost of some loss or inconvenience, for later they may have to be settled at the cost of immense harm and enormous slaughter that cannot even be imagined now. But this peace must be based on justice and freedom for mankind, and must take into account the rights of individuals and communities. Otherwise it will be fluid and unstable. . . .

Statement of the American Roman Catholic Bishops, meeting in Washington, November, 1966

Our common humanity demands that all people live in peace and harmony with one another. This peace will exist only if the right order established by God is observed, an order which is based on the requirement of human dignity. Everyone, therefore, must be vitally and personally concerned about correcting the grave disorders which today threaten peace. As Catholics we are members of the Church which Pope Paul has called a "Messenger of Peace."

We, the Catholic bishops of the United States, consider it our duty to help magnify the moral voice of our nation. This voice, fortunately, is becoming louder and clearer because it is the voice of all faiths. To the strong words of the National Council of Churches, the Synagogue Council of America, and other religious bodies, we add our own plea for peace. Our approaches may at times differ, but our starting point (justice) and our goal (peace) do not.

While we cannot resolve all the issues involved in the Vietnam conflict, it is clearly our duty to insist that they be kept under constant moral scrutiny. No one is free to evade his personal responsibility by leaving it entirely to others to make moral judgments. In this connection, the Vatican Council warns that "men should take heed not to entrust themselves only to the efforts of others, while remaining careless about their own attitudes. For government officials, who must simultaneously guarantee the good of their own people and promote the universal good, depend on public opinion and feeling to the greatest possible extent."

Peace and Modern Warfare

While it is not possible in this brief statement to give a detailed analysis of the Church's total teaching on war and peace, it seems necessary to review certain basic principles if the present crisis is to be put in its proper moral perspectives.

We reaffirmed at the council the legitimate role of patriotism for the well-being of a nation, but a clear distinction was made between true and false patriotism: "Citizens should develop a generous and loyal devotion to their country, but without any narrowing of mind. In other words, they must always look simultaneously to the welfare of the whole human family, which is tied together by the manifold bonds linking races, peoples and nations."

But these limits on patriotism do not rule out a country's right to legitimate self-defense. While making it clear that all means short of force must first be used, the council restated the traditional teaching regarding the right of self-defense: "As long as the danger of war remains and there is no competent and sufficiently powerful authority at the international level, government cannot be denied the right to legitimate defense." And what a nation can do to defend itself, it may do to help another in its struggle against aggression.

In the conduct of any war, there must be moral limits: "Any act of war aimed indiscriminately at the destruction of entire cities or of extensive areas along with their population is a crime against God and man himself. It merits univocal and unhesitating condemnation." Moreover, as the council also reminded us the fact that a war of self-defense has unhappily begun does not mean that any and all means may be employed by the warring parties.

While the stockpiling of scientific weapons serves, for the present, as a deterrent to aggression, the council has warned us that "the arms race in which so many countries are engaged is not a safe way to preserve a steady peace." Indeed, it is a "treacherous trap for humanity." Far from promoting a sure and authentic peace, it actually fosters war by diverting resources which could be better used to alleviate the human misery which causes war. In their urgent plea for disarmament, however, the council fathers understood that it will be effective only if it is universal and if there are adequate means of enforcing it.

The council commended those citizens who defend their nation against aggression. They are "instruments of security and freedom on behalf of their people. As long as they fulfill this role properly, they are making a genuine contribution to the establishment of peace." At the same time, however, it pointed out that some provision should be made for those who conscientiously object to bearing arms: "It seems right that laws make humane provisions for the care of those who for reasons of conscience refuse to bear arms; provided, however, that they accept some other form of service to the human community."

Principles Put to Work

In the light of these principles, how are we as Americans to judge the involvement of the United States in Vietnam? What can we do to promote peace?

Americans can have confidence in the sincerity of their leaders as long as they work for a just peace in Vietnam. Their efforts to find a solution to the present impasse are well known. We realize that citizens of all faiths and of differing political loyalties honestly differ among themselves over the moral issues involved in this tragic conflict. While we do not claim to be able to resolve these issues authoritatively, in the light of the facts as they are known to us, it is reasonable to argue that our presence in Vietnam is justified. We share the anguish of our government officials in their awesome responsibility of making life-and-death decisions about our national policy in Vietnam. We commend the valor of our men in the armed forces, and we express to them our debt of gratitude. In our time, thousands of men have given their lives in war. To those who loved them, we express our sorrow at their loss and promise our constant prayer.

But we cannot stop here. While we can conscientiously support the position of our country in the present circumstances, it is the duty of everyone to search for other alternatives. And everyone—government leaders and citizens alike—must be prepared to change our course whenever a change in circumstances warrants it.

This can be done effectively only if we know the facts and issues involved. Within the limits imposed by our national security, therefore, we must always insist that these facts and issues be made known to the public so that they can be considered in their moral context.

On the basis of our knowledge and understanding of the current situation, we are also bound always to make sure that our government does, in fact, pursue every possibility which offers even the slightest hope of a peaceful settlement. And we must always clearly protest whenever there is a danger that the conflict will be escalated beyond morally acceptable limits.

On a broader level, we must support our government in its efforts to negotiate a workable formula for disarmament. What we seek is not unilateral disarmament, but one proceeding, in the words of the council, "at an equal pace according to agreement, and backed up by authentic and workable safeguards." We commend the officials of our country and others for their contribution to the proposed Treaty Against Nuclear Proliferation which, hopefully, will soon become a reality.

Moreover, we must use every resource available as a nation, to help alleviate the basic causes of war. If the God-given human dignity of the people of poorer nations is not to become an illusion, these nations must be able to provide for the spiritual and material needs of their citizens. We must help them do this. The economically developed nations of the world, as Pope John insisted in his great encyclical, *Pacem in Terris,* must come to the aid of those which are in process of developing so that every man, woman and child in the world may be able "to live in conditions more in keeping with their human dignity."

"THE SECOND MILE"

There is a grave danger that the circumstances of the present war in Vietnam may, in time, diminish our moral sensitivity to its evils. Every means at our disposal, therefore, must be used to create a climate of peace. In this climate, prayer, personal example, study, discussion and lectures can strengthen the will for peace. We must advocate what we believe are the best methods of promoting peace: mutual agreement, safeguards and inspection; the creation of an international public authority to negotiate toward peace. Above all, in its peace-making efforts, we must support the work of the United Nations which, in the words of Pope Paul, marks "a stage in the development of mankind, from which retreat must never be admitted, but from which it is necessary that advance be made."

We ask every person of good will to support with prayer the Holy Father's plea for a Christmas cease-fire. May it open the way to lasting peace. In the spirit of Christ, the Christian must be the persistent seeker in the Gospel, the man willing to walk the second mile (cf. Matt. 5:42). He walks prudently, but he walks generously and he asks that all men do the same.

As Catholics we walk in good company. Pope Paul, in his recent encyclical on peace, cried out in God's name, to stop war. We pray God that the sacrifices of us all, our prayers as well as our faltering efforts toward peace, will hasten the day when the whole world will echo Pope Paul's historic words: "No more war, war never again!"

Excerpts from
"An Appeal to the Churches Concerning Vietnam,"
issued by the General Assembly
of the National Council of Churches
December 9, 1966

(*Note:* The early portions of the text discussed (1) the scope and importance in the Vietnam war, (2) the need for flexibility and openness in the present situation, (3) the use of military power in Vietnam, (4) the need for international responsibility in securing peace and (5) the need for development and reconciliation. After these considerations, the text concluded as follows:)

ASSEMBLY STATEMENTS

In the light of these considerations concerning the extent and danger of the Vietnam war, and in the light of our conviction that the war must end soon, the General Assembly makes the following statements:

[1]

Knowing that God commands us in every situation to seek the truth, and remembering the best in the U.S. tradition of freedom of speech, we record our conviction that widespread debate concerning the complex situation in Vietnam is not disloyal either to the nation or to our troops there, but on the contrary is a primary means of helping to secure peace and justice in Vietnam.

[2]

We ask for more candor on the part of those who make Government policy in relation to Vietnam as an indispensable step in securing enlightened public relations in the U.S.A. and in securing peace in Vietnam.

In particular, we ask for more candor as regards the following: The efforts of the Government to negotiate and the replies to them; the efforts of the Government to move the Vietnam conflict into the sphere of multilateral judgment and responsibility; the willingness of the Government to negotiate with the National Liberation Front; basic military policy, and within the limits of necessary security, whether increased escalation and to what approximate degree, or leveling off, or de-escalation; willingness to arrange for a phased withdrawal of U.S. forces under international supervision.

[3]

We urge, for reasons given in Sections 3 and 4 of the foregoing statement, that the judgment, responsibility and action of the United Nations be sought by placing the issue of the Vietnam conflict on its agenda in a manner which will further the initiative of the Secretary General, in the absence of reasonable assurance that the Geneva Conference will be convened shortly or that hostilities will be brought to an end by other means. In our judgment, this should be accompanied by:

(a) Readiness on the part of the U.S.A. to support the

United Nations in negotiations "for a cease-fire agreement (including cessation of terrorist activities) under United Nations supervision, among the governments of the United States, of North and South Vietnam and other interested parties, including representatives from the National Liberation Front; such negotiations are imperative and may be possible on the basis of the mutual interest of sparing the population further and frightful suffering." (General Board, Dec. 1965).

(b) Readiness on the part of the U.S.A. to support the United Nations in negotiations with all interested governments and the National Liberation Front.

(c) Readiness on the part of the United States Government to give the most serious consideration to a halt in the bombing of North Vietnam even though there may be no advance assurance of reciprocal action by the North Vietnamese Government.

The Secretary General of the United Nations has proposed a halt to the bombing of North Vietnam as the first step in an effort to end the hostilities and begin negotiations. Such action would be most timely in the light of the agreed holiday truce and Pope Paul's appeals for a prolongation of that truce. It would be especially appropriate as a humanitarian expression of our celebration of the coming of the Prince of Peace.

(d) Readiness to "make clear that a primary objective of a settlement of the Vietnam conflict is the independence of South Vietnam from outside interference, with complete liberty to determine the character of its future government by the result of a peaceful, free verified choice of its people." (General Board, Dec. 1965).

(e) Readiness to agree to "a phased withdrawal of all its troops and bases from the Vietnamese territory, if and when they can be replaced by adequate international peace-keeping forces, composed of military contingents capable of maintaining order while the peace settlement is being carried out." (General Board, Dec. 1965).

[4]

For reasons indicated in the foregoing statement we ask that the U.S. Government make available, through Congress, in fulfillment of the President's proposal, immediate reconstruction assistance and long-range economic development funds for Southeast Asia, including the several associated states of Indochina—this aid to be made available preferably through an effective international organization in which the beneficiary governments fully participate.

[5]

We urge all to join in continual prayer—for our country, for the people of Vietnam, for all engaged in military action, for the peace of the world and for the reconciliation of all God's people.

REQUESTS TO CHURCHES

In the light of the great importance of these issues, it is urgent that the religious communities vigorously discharge their responsibility for developing the moral and spiritual climate needed to prepare the paths of peace in at least the following ways:

(a) The General Assembly asks the churches to mount a major effort to expand their study, debate and action concerning these issues within their own constituencies and cooperatively.

The General Assembly therefore asks the churches, the councils of churches, organizations of church men, women, youth and students to join in the total effort. The General Assembly directs the N.C.C.U.S.A. to provide initiative and support to the churches and related organizations in their witness in regard to Vietnam.

(b) The General Assembly considers this appeal to be of the utmost urgency. The General Assembly acknowledges the contribution made by the recent statement of the National Conference of Catholic Bishops, and agrees with the conference that it is "our duty to help magnify the moral voice of our nation."

To that end, the General Assembly expresses its hope that the Protestant, Orthodox and Roman Catholic communities, together with the Jewish community, may more closely collaborate in helping to create the climate in which justice and peace in Vietnam may be secured.

To keep the Vietnam war under constant moral scrutiny,

widespread study, discussion and action are required. Much of this can and should be done together with each religious community adhering to its own convictions. Thus, may we join in our plea for peace, and express our common will for peace.

Selected Bibliography

Books

Gettleman, Marvin E., ed. *Vietnam: History, Documents and Opinions on a Major World Crisis.* Greenwich: Fawcett Publications, Inc., 1965.

Raskin, Marcus G., and Fall, Bernard B., eds. *The Viet-Nam Reader: Articles and Documents on American Foreign Policy and the Viet-Nam Crisis.* New York: Vintage Books, 1965.

These two paperbacks contain all the primary source materials necessary for one who wishes to become informed about the tangled history of America's increasing involvement in Vietnam.

* * *

Bennett, John C. *Foreign Policy in Christian Perspective.* New York: Scribner's, 1966.

Helpful background and perspective on the broader context of foreign policy in which Vietnam must be viewed.

Burchett, Wilfred G. *Viet-Nam: Inside Story of the Guerilla War.* New York: International Publishers, 1965.

A pro-Communist report by an Australian Communist.

Fall, Bernard B. *The Two Viet-Nams: A Political and Military History.* New York: Praeger, 1965.

———. *Viet-Nam Witness.* New York: Praeger, 1966.

Interpretive treatments by one of the best-informed scholars, who was recently killed by a land mine in Vietnam.

Friends, Society of. *Peace in Vietnam: A New Approach in Southeast Asia.* New York: Hill & Wang, 1966.

A report prepared for the American Friends Service Committee.

Fullbright, J. William. *The Arrogance of Power.* New York: Vintage Books, 1967.

An overall view of American politics by the most consistent critic of Administration policy in Vietnam. Chapters 5, 6, 7, and 9 are particularly relevant to Vietnam, the latter offering an eight-point alternative to our present policy.

Goodwin, Richard N. *Triumph or Tragedy: Reflections on Vietnam.* New York: Vintage Books, 1965.
An account of our dilemma written by a former adviser to Presidents Kennedy and Johnson.

Greene, Felix. *Vietnam! Vietnam!* Palo Alto: Fulton, 1966.
A poignant book of photographs indicating the cost of the war in terms of human suffering.

Halberstam, David. *The Making of a Quagmire.* New York: Random House, 1965.
Pulitzer-prize-winning account of the events from 1961 to 1964, with special attention to the fall of the Diem regime.

Kahin, George M., and Lewis, John W. *The United States in Vietnam.* New York: Dell Publishing Co., 1967.
Probably the best single account.

Lacouture, Jean. *Vietnam: Between Two Truces,* trans. K. Kellen and J. Carmichael. New York: Vintage Books, 1966.
A non-American perspective on the war by a correspondent for *Le Monde.*

Pike, Douglas. *Viet Cong.* Cambridge: M.I.T. Press, 1966.
The best-informed source about Vietnamese documents and organizations.

Schlesinger, Arthur M., Jr. *The Bitter Heritage: Vietnam and American Democracy 1941-1966.* Boston: Houghton Mifflin Co., 1967.
A brief and eminently readable treatment of the history of American involvement, with proposals for a "middle course" of action to replace our present policy.

Schurmann, Franz, Scott, Peter D., and Zelnik, Reginald. *The Politics of Escalation in Vietnam.* Boston: Beacon Press, 1966, and Greenwich: Fawcett Publications, Inc., 1966.
A "citizen's white paper" indicating how the American response to peace feelers from the other side has been a consistent policy of military escalation.

Trager, Frank N. *Why Vietnam?* New York: Praeger, 1966.
A statement supporting the Administration position.

Articles

Carver, George A., Jr. "The Real Revolution in South Vietnam," *Foreign Affairs,* April, 1965.

Chomsky, Noam. "The Responsibility of Intellectuals," *The New York Review of Books,* February 23, 1967.

Draper, Theodore. "The American Crisis: Vietnam, Cuba and the Dominican Republic," *Commentary,* January, 1967.
Particularly recommended.

Fall, Bernard B., Goodwin, Richard N., McGovern, George,

and Roche, John P. "Containing China," *Commentary*, May, 1966.

Gass, Oscar. "Vietnam—Resistance or Withdrawal?" *Commentary*, May, 1964.

Gellhorn, Martha. "Suffer the Little Children," *Ladies' Home Journal*, January, 1967.

Deals with injuries sustained by children as a result of American use of napalm.

Gottlieb, Sanford. "The Road to Negotiations," *Saturday Review*, December 18, 1965.

Lansdale, Edward G. "Vietnam: Do We Understand Revolution?" *Foreign Affairs*, October, 1964.

Lichtheim, George. "The Cold War in Perspective," *Commentary*, June, 1964.

Pepper, William. "The Children of Vietnam," *Ramparts*, January, 1967.

Deals with injuries sustained by children as a result of American use of napalm.

Schoenbrun, David. "Vietnam: The Case for Extrication," *Christianity and Crisis*, February 6, 1967.

Schwartz, Benjamin. "Chinese Visions and American Policies, *Commentary*, April, 1966.

Sheehan, Neil. "Not A Dove, But No Longer A Hawk," *New York Times Magazine*, October 9, 1966.

"Vietnam: A First Step," editorial, *The Saturday Evening Post*, February 11, 1967.